Dissolved Oxygen Analysis, TMDL Model Comparison, and Particulate Matter Shunting: Preliminary Results from Three Model Scenarios for the Klamath River Upstream of Keno Dam, Oregon

By Annett B. Sullivan and Stewart A. Rounds, U.S. Geological Survey; Michael L. Deas and I. Ertugrul Sogutlugil, Watercourse Engineering, Inc.

Prepared in cooperation with the Bureau of Reclamation

Open-File Report 2012–1101

U.S. Department of the Interior
U.S. Geological Survey

U.S. Department of the Interior
KEN SALAZAR, Secretary

U.S. Geological Survey
Marcia K. McNutt, Director

U.S. Geological Survey, Reston, Virginia: 2012

For more information on the USGS—the Federal source for science about the Earth,
its natural and living resources, natural hazards, and the environment,
visit http://www.usgs.gov or call 1–888–ASK–USGS.

For an overview of USGS information products, including maps, imagery, and publications,
visit http://www.usgs.gov/pubprod

To order this and other USGS information products, visit http://store.usgs.gov

Suggested citation:
Sullivan, A.B., Rounds, S.A., Deas, M.L., and Sogutlugil, I.E., 2012, Dissolved oxygen analysis, TMDL model
comparison, and particulate matter shunting—Preliminary results from three model scenarios for the Klamath
River upstream of Keno Dam, Oregon: U.S. Geological Survey Open-File Report 2012-1101, 30 p.

Contents

Significant Findings 1

Background 3

Purpose and Scope 5

Model Description..5

Model Scenarios 6

    Scenario 3. Compliance with Dissolved Oxygen Standards, Before and After TMDL Implementation. 7

        Dissolved Oxygen Standards...7

        Natural Conditions Dissolved Oxygen..8

        Scenario Setup 9

        Results of Scenario 3 Analyses 10

            Depth-Averaged vs. Volume-Averaged Dissolved Oxygen Concentrations 10

            Natural Conditions Dissolved Oxygen Effect on the Standard...11

            Comparison to the Dissolved Oxygen Standard 13

            Representativeness of the Seven ODEQ Compliance Locations 16

    Scenario 4. Comparison of the USGS and TMDL Models Using 2006–09 Data 17

        Scenario Setup 17

        Results of Scenario 4 Analyses 18

    Scenario 5. Shunting Particulate Material from Diversion Canals into the Klamath River......................21

        Particulate Shunting..22

        Changes to Return-Flow Concentrations 23

        Results of Scenario 5 Analyses 24

Acknowledgments 27

References Cited 27

Appendix—Code Changes to CE-QUAL-W2 29

    A. Natural Conditions Code Changes 29

    B. Particulate Matter Shunting Code Changes 30

Figures

Figure 1. Map showing location of the study area, streamflow-gaging stations, and point-source inputs in the upper Klamath River, Oregon...4

Figure 2. Graph showing Upper Klamath Lake and Link River total phosphorus TMDL targets and natural conditions Link River total phosphorus for the USGS and TMDL models. 9

Figure 3. Graphs showing comparison of volume-averaged and depth-averaged dissolved oxygen concentration for calendar year 2008 at model segment 38, the Miller Island monitoring site..11

Figure 4. Graphs showing base case [3(1a)] and natural conditions [3(nc)] scenarios for 2008 dissolved oxygen concentration at Miller Island (model segment 38) in the Link River to Keno reach of the Klamath River, and the relevant dissolved oxygen standards. 12

Figure 5. Graphs showing (A) minimum 30-day mean dissolved oxygen concentration at each modeled location during 2007 for scenario 3 model runs and (B) the difference between that minimum 30-day mean dissolved oxygen and the dissolved oxygen standard relevant for that location and day. 15

Figure 6. Graph showing number of days dissolved oxygen concentrations at all modeled locations in the Link River to Keno Dam reach violated the dissolved oxygen standard in the 2007 base case (scenario 1a)........17

Figure 7a. Graphs showing comparison of year 2007 measured algae, total nitrogen, particulate nitrogen, nitrate, and ammonia data, calibrated model results, and scenario 4 (2007 inputs applied to TMDL model setup) results for sites in the Klamath River upstream of Keno Dam, Oregon. 19

Figure 7b. Graphs showing comparison of year 2007 measured total phosphorus, orthophosphorus, particulate organic carbon, dissolved organic carbon, and dissolved oxygen data, calibrated model results, and scenario 4 (2007 inputs applied to TMDL model setup) results for sites in the Klamath River upstream of Keno Dam, Oregon. 20

Figure 8. Graph showing flows for A Canal, Lost River Diversion Channel, North Canal, Ady Canal, and Klamath Straits Drain for 2007. 22

Figure 9. Graph showing particulate organic load (particulate organic material + algae) at Link River for 2006 under current conditions and under A Canal particulate shunting. 23

Figure 10. Graph showing 30-day mean dissolved oxygen concentrations at model segment 78 (site KRS12a) for the base case and scenarios 5a, 5b, 5c, and 5d in 2008.. 26

Tables

Table 1. Model scenarios for the Link River to Keno Dam reach of the Klamath River, Oregon 6

Table 2. Number of days the Klamath River would violate dissolved oxygen standards at the seven ODEQ compliance locations for base case and TMDL compliance scenarios for years 2006–09 13

Table 3. Number of days the Klamath River would violate dissolved oxygen standards at the seven ODEQ compliance locations in the base case and particulate shunting scenarios for years 2006–09. 25

Conversion Factors, Datums, and Abbreviations and Acronyms

Conversion Factors

Inch/Pound to SI

Multiply	By	To obtain
foot (ft)	0.3048	meter (m)
mile (mi)	1.609	kilometer (km)
cubic foot per second (ft^3/s)	0.02832	cubic meter per second (m^3/s)

SI to Inch/Pound

Multiply	By	To obtain
meter (m)	3.281	foot (ft)

Temperature in degrees Celsius (°C) may be converted to degrees Fahrenheit (°F) as follows: °F=(1.8×°C)+32.

Specific conductance is given in microsiemens per centimeter at 25 degrees Celsius (μS/cm at 25 °C).

Concentrations of chemical constituents in water are given in milligrams per liter (mg/L), which is approximately equivalent to parts per million (ppm), or micrograms per liter (μg/L), which is approximately equivalent to parts per billion (ppb).

Datums

Vertical coordinate information is referenced to the Upper Klamath Lake Vertical Datum (UKLVD), established by the Bureau of Reclamation. For this report, the conversion is UKLVD − 1.78 ft = National Geodetic Vertical Datum of 1929 (NGVD29).

Horizontal coordinate information is referenced to the North American Datum of 1983 (NAD 83).

"Elevation" refers to distance above the vertical datum.

Dissolved Oxygen Analysis, TMDL Model Comparison, and Particulate Matter Shunting: Preliminary Results from Three Model Scenarios for the Klamath River Upstream of Keno Dam, Oregon

By Annett B. Sullivan and Stewart A. Rounds, U.S. Geological Survey; Michael L. Deas and I. Ertugrul Sogutlugil, Watercourse Engineering, Inc.

Significant Findings

Efforts are underway to identify actions that would improve water quality in the Link River to Keno Dam reach of the Upper Klamath River in south-central Oregon. To provide further insight into water-quality improvement options, three scenarios were developed, run, and analyzed using previously calibrated CE-QUAL-W2 hydrodynamic and water-quality models. Additional scenarios are under development as part of this ongoing study. Most of these scenarios evaluate changes relative to a "current conditions" model, but in some cases a "natural conditions" model was used that simulated the reach without the effect of point and nonpoint sources and set Upper Klamath Lake at its Total Maximum Daily Load (TMDL) targets. These scenarios were simulated using a model developed by the U.S. Geological Survey (USGS) and Watercourse Engineering, Inc. for the years 2006–09, referred to here as the "USGS model." Another model of the reach was developed by Tetra Tech, Inc. for years 2000 and 2002 to support the Klamath River TMDL process; that model is referred to here as the "TMDL model."

The three scenarios described in this report included (1) an analysis of whether this reach of the Upper Klamath River would be in compliance with dissolved oxygen standards if sources met TMDL allocations, (2) an application of more recent datasets to the TMDL model with comparison to results from the USGS model, and (3) an examination of the effect on dissolved oxygen in the Klamath River if particulate material were stopped from entering Klamath Project diversion canals. Updates and modifications to the USGS model are in progress, so in the future these scenarios will be reanalyzed with the updated model and the interim results presented here will be superseded. Significant findings from this phase of the investigation include:

- The TMDL analysis used depth-averaged dissolved oxygen concentrations from model output for comparison with dissolved oxygen standards. The Oregon dissolved oxygen standards do not specify whether the numeric criteria are based on depth-averaged dissolved oxygen concentration; this was an interpretation of the standards rule by the Oregon Department of Environmental Quality (ODEQ). In this study, both depth-averaged and volume-averaged dissolved oxygen concentrations were calculated from model output. Results showed that modeled depth-averaged concentrations typically were lower than volume-averaged dissolved oxygen concentrations because depth-averaging gives a higher weight to small volume areas near the channel bottom that often have lower dissolved oxygen concentrations. Results from model scenarios in this study are reported using volume-averaged dissolved oxygen concentrations.

- Under all scenarios analyzed, violations of the dissolved oxygen standard occurred most often in summer. Of the three dissolved oxygen criteria that must be met, the 30-day standard was violated most frequently. Under the base case (current conditions), fewer violations occurred in the upstream part of the reach. More violations occurred in the downstream direction, due in part to oxygen demand from the decay of algae and organic matter from Link River and other inflows.

- A condition in which Upper Klamath Lake and its Link River outflow achieved Upper Klamath Lake TMDL water-quality targets was most effective in reducing the number of violations of the dissolved oxygen standard in the Link River to Keno Dam reach of the Klamath River. The condition in which point and nonpoint sources within the Link River to Keno Dam reach met Klamath River TMDL allocations had no effect on dissolved oxygen compliance in some locations and a small effect in others under current conditions. On the other hand, meeting TMDL allocations for nonpoint and point sources was predicted to be important in meeting dissolved oxygen criteria when Upper Klamath Lake and Link River also met Upper Klamath TMDL water-quality targets.

- The location of greatest dissolved oxygen improvement from nutrient and organic matter reductions was downstream from point and nonpoint source inflows because time and distance are required for decay to occur and for oxygen demand to be exerted.

- After assessing compliance with dissolved oxygen standards at all 102 model segments in the Link River to Keno Dam reach, it was determined that the seven locations used by ODEQ appear to be a representative subset of the reach for dissolved oxygen analysis.

- The USGS and TMDL models were qualitatively compared by running both models for the 2006–09 period but preserving the essential characteristics of each, such as organic matter partitioning, bathymetric representation, and parameter rates. The analysis revealed that some constituents were not greatly affected by the differing algorithms, rates, and assumptions in the two models. Conversely, other constituents, especially organic matter, were simulated differently by the two models. Organic matter in this river system is best represented by a mixture of relatively labile particulate material and a substantial concentration of refractory dissolved material. In addition, the use of a first-order sediment oxygen demand, as in the USGS model, helps to capture the seasonal and dynamic effect of settled organic and algal material.

- Simulation of shunting (diverting) particulate material away from the intake of four Klamath Project diversion canals, so that the material stayed in the river and out of the Project area, caused higher concentrations of particulate material to occur in the river. In all cases modeled, the increase in in-river particulate material also produced decreased dissolved oxygen concentrations and an increase in the number of days when dissolved oxygen standards were violated.

- If particulate material were shunted back into the river at the Klamath Project diversion canals, less organic matter and nutrients would be taken into the Klamath Project area and the Lost River basin, resulting in return flows to the Klamath River via Lost River Diversion Channel that may have reduced nutrient concentrations. Model scenarios bracketing potential end-member nutrient concentrations showed that the composition of the return flows had little to no effect on dissolved oxygen compliance under simulated conditions.

Background

The Klamath River flows about 255 mi (410 km) from the outlet of Upper Klamath Lake through southern Oregon and northern California to the Pacific Ocean. The first 21 mi of the river, just downstream of Upper Klamath Lake, are bounded by Link River Dam and Keno Dam (fig. 1). Water quality in this reach has been classified as "very poor" by the State of Oregon (Mrazik, 2007) and was designated as "water quality limited" on Oregon's 303(d) list for exceeding ammonia toxicity and dissolved oxygen criteria year-round, and pH and chlorophyll *a* criteria in summer (Oregon Department of Environmental Quality, 2007). A TMDL for the Klamath River was submitted to the Environmental Protection Agency (EPA) in December 2010 (Oregon Department of Environmental Quality, 2010). In the TMDL, load reductions of total nitrogen, total phosphorus, and biochemical oxygen demand (BOD) were specified for the nonpoint sources Lost River Diversion Channel and Klamath Straits Drain and for point sources Klamath Falls wastewater treatment plant and South Suburban wastewater treatment plant. For example, the TMDL would require greater than 80-percent reductions in total nitrogen, total phosphorus, and BOD in the Lost River Diversion Channel and Klamath Straits Drain.

As a foundation for the TMDL process, ODEQ and Tetra Tech, Inc. developed a water-quality model for the Klamath River, including the Link River to Keno Dam (Link to Keno) reach, based on a model previously developed for a dam-relicensing process by Watercourse Engineering, Inc. (Watercourse Engineering, Inc., 2004). For the Link to Keno reach, a modified CE-QUAL-W2 model was constructed and calibrated for the years 2000 and 2002 (Tetra Tech, Inc., 2009). The datasets used to drive the model, however, did not include direct measurements of organic matter concentrations, organic matter partitioning, or algae species. The technical basis of the TMDL model for the Link to Keno reach was reviewed and evaluated by the USGS (Rounds and Sullivan, 2009 and 2010).

Beginning in 2006, the USGS began a collaboration with the Bureau of Reclamation (Reclamation) and Watercourse Engineering, Inc. (Watercourse) to collect detailed datasets, conduct research, and develop a new water-quality model for the Link to Keno reach of the Klamath River. The goal was to produce a model that accurately represented the most important instream processes affecting water quality so that potential management strategies could be evaluated and prioritized. The result was a CE-QUAL-W2 model calibrated for 2006–09 conditions that simulated three separate algal groups and relied on recent research and measurements to characterize the instream processes controlling water quality in the Klamath River (Sullivan and others, 2011). The model simulates water velocity, streamflow, stage, temperature, and a wide range of water-quality constituents including algae, nutrients, organic matter, suspended sediment, and dissolved oxygen. Based on extensive field data (Sullivan and others, 2008, 2009) and experimental studies on flow, suspended-matter settling, and dissolved oxygen and organic matter dynamics (Sullivan and others, 2010; Poulson and Sullivan, 2010; Deas and Vaughn, 2011), the USGS-Watercourse-Reclamation model (henceforth simply called the USGS model) of the Link to Keno reach has a sound technical basis for the exploration of a range of management strategies.

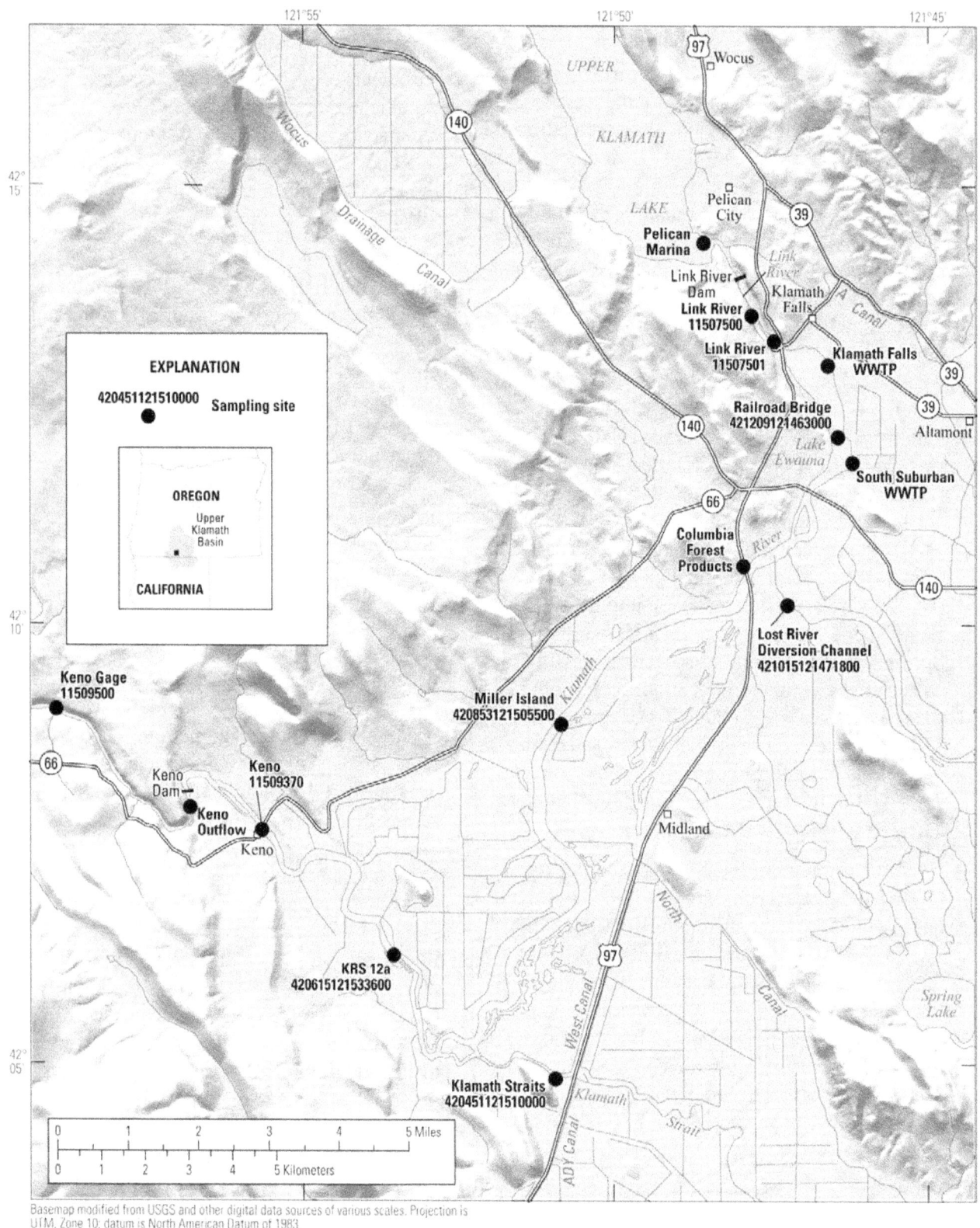

Figure 1. Map showing location of the study area, streamflow-gaging stations, and point-source inputs in the upper Klamath River, Oregon.

Purpose and Scope

The purpose of this report is to present the results of using the USGS and TMDL CE-QUAL-W2 models of the Link to Keno reach of the Klamath River to analyze three new model scenarios (numbered 3 through 5). Two model scenarios (numbered 1 and 2) were run and analyzed previously (Sullivan and others, 2011). Those two scenarios investigated Klamath River water-quality changes that might occur if UpperKlamath Lake and Upper Klamath River point and nonpoint inflows were to meet their respective TMDL allocations. The three model scenarios run and evaluated for this report include:

3. Compliance with dissolved oxygen standards, before and after TMDL implementation (USGS model).

4. Comparison of the USGS and TMDL models using 2006–09 data (simulations of current conditions).

5. Shunting particulate material from Klamath Project diversion canals into the Klamath River, such that particulate material that normally would be withdrawn remains instead in the Klamath River (USGS model).

The USGS model for years 2006–09 for this reach is currently being refined in two ways: (1) incorporation of dissolved organic matter, phosphoric acid, and ammonia buffering into the pH subroutine and (2) inclusion of macrophytes (rooted aquatic plants) in the model based on data collected in summer 2011. Thus, the scenarios presented in this report are interim results because all model scenarios will be rerun with the updated model when those modifications are finalized. Additional model scenarios, currently in development, will also be run with the updated model. The purpose of this report is to publish some of these interim results in a timely manner so that the results can be considered as part of an ongoing resource management and planning process.

Model Description

The concentration of a constituent in a river can be affected by hydrology, atmospheric conditions, tributary inputs, withdrawals, chemical reactions, and biochemical reactions and processes. Mechanistic, sometimes called physically based, computer models include many of these processes and are regularly used to make predictions about effects on water quality in response to system changes. The models used in this study were built with the mechanistic model CE-QUAL-W2, a two-dimensional, laterally averaged, hydrodynamic, water temperature, and water-quality model (Cole and Wells, 2008). CE-QUAL-W2 has been applied to hundreds of lakes, reservoirs, and rivers around the world with good success.

The USGS-constructed Upper Klamath River CE-QUAL-W2 model for 2006–09 simulates flow, water temperature, specific conductance, dissolved and suspended solids, dissolved oxygen, total nitrogen, ammonia, nitrate, total phosphorus, orthophosphate, dissolved and particulate organic matter, and three algal groups: blue-greens, diatoms, and other algae (Sullivan and others, 2011). A similar set of constituents was included in the TMDL model. Both the USGS and TMDL models can simulate these constituents from the mouth of Link River to Keno Dam. The USGS model grid is formed from 102 segments that connect together in the direction of flow. Segments average 1,009 ft (308 m) in length and each segment represents a cross-sectional shape with stacked rectangular layers of varying width from the river surface to the channel bottom. Grid layers were all 0.61 m in height; since CE-QUAL-W2 allows for a variable water surface elevation, water in the uppermost layer may be lower than the maximum layer height. The model produces output for all constituents for each layer of each segment at a chosen time interval, often hourly.

Although the models were constructed and calibrated for current conditions, the mechanistic nature of the models allows them to make useful predictions of hydrodynamic, thermal, and water-quality changes resulting from altered conditions. It is important to remember, however, that all model predictions have some uncertainty. Model scenario results are most useful in providing insights regarding changes to the system, rather than providing high certainty regarding the values of predicted concentrations; for example, model results can be used to evaluate decisions about which treatment or restoration processes might be most effective at improving water quality by assessing the predicted changes in key constituent concentrations.

Model Scenarios

The calibrated Link-Keno model was used to set up, run, and analyze three scenarios (table 1, scenarios 3 to 5). All scenarios were run for model years 2006–09 to examine a range of possible effects under different flow, meteorological, and water-quality conditions. Previously run scenarios 1 and 2 examined changes in Upper Klamath River water quality under conditions in which Upper Klamath River point and nonpoint sources met Klamath River TMDL allocations, and/or Upper Klamath Lake and its Link River outflow achieved water-quality targets of the Upper Klamath Lake TMDL (Sullivan and others, 2011). Outlined herein are scenario assumptions, conditions, and associated information as well as results for scenarios 3 through 5.

Table 1. Model scenarios for the Link River to Keno Dam reach of the Klamath River, Oregon·

[Scenarios were run for calendar years 2006–09. Scenario 3 is based upon further analyses of Scenarios 1 and 2. Abbreviations: TMDL, Total Maximum Daily Load; LRDC, Lost River Diversion Channel; KSD, Klamath Straits Drain; DO, dissolved oxygen; OM, organic matter]

Scenario Number	Description	Results presented
Scenario 1: point and nonpoint tributary sources at TMDL compliance		
1a	Base case (current conditions)	Sullivan and others, 2011
1b	TMDL tributaries	Sullivan and others, 2011
Scenario 2: Link River at TMDL compliance		
2a	TMDL Link River	Sullivan and others, 2011
2b	TMDL Link River and TMDL tributaries	Sullivan and others, 2011
Scenario 3: compliance with dissolved oxygen standards analysis		
3(nc)	Natural conditions, without anthropogenic impact	This report
3(1a)	Base case (current conditions)	This report
3(1b)	TMDL tributaries	This report
3(2a)	TMDL Link River	This report
3(2b)	TMDL Link River and tributaries	This report
Scenario 4: comparison to TMDL model		
4	Apply 2006-09 data to TMDL model	This report

Table 1. Model scenarios for the Link River to Keno Dam reach of the Klamath River, Oregon—continued

[Scenarios were run for calendar years 2006–09. Scenario 3 is based upon further analyses of Scenarios 1 and 2. Abbreviations: TMDL, Total Maximum Daily Load; LRDC, Lost River Diversion Channel; KSD, Klamath Straits Drain; DO, dissolved oxygen; OM, organic matter]

Scenario Number	Description	Results presented
	Scenario 5: particulate matter shunting	
5a	Shunt, LRDC and KSD current	This report
5b	Shunt, LRDC and KSD intermediate	This report
5c	Shunt, LRDC and KSD zero OM, nutrients, and algae, with DO at saturation	This report

Scenario 3. Compliance with Dissolved Oxygen Standards, Before and After TMDL Implementation.

Scenario 3 extends scenario 1 and 2 analyses further, and compares predicted instream dissolved oxygen concentrations to Oregon dissolved oxygen standards under various TMDL attainment conditions.

Dissolved Oxygen Standards

For the Link-Keno reach of the Upper Klamath River, classified as cool-water aquatic habitat, the relevant Oregon dissolved oxygen standard states *"...the dissolved oxygen may not fall below 6.5 mg/L as a 30-day mean minimum, 5.0 mg/L as a 7-day minimum mean, and may not fall below 4.0 mg/L as an absolute minimum"* (Oregon Department of Environmental Quality, 2011). The *"30-day mean minimum"* is defined as the minimum of the 30 consecutive-day floating averages of the calculated daily mean, and the *"7-day minimum mean"* is defined as the minimum of the 7 consecutive-day floating average of the daily minimum concentration. These numeric criteria are superseded if natural conditions are determined to have lower levels of dissolved oxygen; in that case, the natural conditions dissolved oxygen concentration becomes the standard. Additional applicable rule language for this reach states that *"no measurable reduction of dissolved oxygen"* shall occur when the numeric criteria are violated, where *"measurable reduction"* is defined as *"...no more than 0.20 mg/L for all anthropogenic activity."* This 0.20

mg/L rule was one of the primary measures used during the determination of allocations for point and nonpoint sources for the Klamath River TMDL (Daniel Turner, ODEQ, oral commun.). Modeled compliance with these dissolved oxygen standards is checked by ODEQ at seven locations within the Link-Keno reach: at the inflows of the Klamath Falls wastewater treatment plant (USGS model segment 4), South Suburban wastewater treatment plant (segment 8), Lost River Diversion Channel (segment 19), and Klamath Straits Drain (model segment 69), as well as at monitoring sites Miller Island (segment 38), KRS12a (segment 78), and Keno (segment 95) (fig. 1).

For TMDL dissolved oxygen analysis in this reach, depth-averaged dissolved oxygen concentrations from model output were calculated in order to compare to dissolved oxygen standards (oral commun., Daniel Turner, ODEQ). The Oregon dissolved oxygen standards rules do not specify any type of depth- or volume-averaging to be used in rivers that are not vertically well mixed; the depth-averaging model output was an interpretation of the dissolved oxygen standards rules by ODEQ. In this study, model depth-averaged dissolved oxygen concentrations were compared to another type of averaging, volume-averaged concentrations. Calculation of depth-averaged dissolved oxygen concentrations from model output assigns equal weight to layers near the channel bottom and near the surface, despite the fact that the wider widths near the water surface contain more water volume than do the bottom layers. Volume-averaged concentrations, on the other hand, account for the cross-sectional width of each layer in the calculation. Both calculations took into account the fact that the total water depth varied over time in the grid.

The instantaneous criterion (4.0 mg/L) was compared to hourly average dissolved oxygen concentrations. The 7-day minimum mean criterion (5.0 mg/L) was compared to the average of the daily minimum of the previous 7 days. For the 30-day mean criterion (6.5 mg/L), the Oregon rules state that *"... for the purpose of calculating the mean, concentrations in excess of 100 percent of saturation are valued at the saturation concentration..."*, so any supersaturated hourly average dissolved oxygen concentrations were set to saturation, and then the average of the daily mean of the previous 30 days was compared to the 6.5 mg/L criterion.

Natural Conditions Dissolved Oxygen

Because the natural conditions dissolved oxygen concentration becomes the dissolved oxygen standard if it is lower than any of the three numeric criteria, it was necessary to set up and run a natural conditions model scenario. ODEQ defines natural conditions as *"conditions or circumstances affecting the physical, chemical, or biological integrity of a water of the state that are not influenced by past or present anthropogenic activities"* (Oregon Department of Environmental Quality, 2011). Anthropogenic activity that modified flow began in this basin before 1900; for instance, the connection between the historical Lower Klamath Lake and the Lost River Slough was closed with a dike in 1890 (Bureau of Reclamation, 2005). Although observational information exists on the nature of flow before anthropogenic activity (Bureau of Reclamation, 2005), some of those observational reports conflict (Weddell, 2000), and little quantitative flow data and no nutrient or organic matter concentration data exist from the time before anthropogenic activity.

Natural conditions models were constructed for both the TMDL modeling and the USGS modeling reported here. In general, both were constructed considering some level of improved water quality imported from Upper Klamath Lake, and limited effects from point and nonpoint source water quality. There were, however, differences in the details of the construction and implementation of the TMDL and USGS natural conditions models.

The construction of the natural conditions TMDL model has been documented and reviewed elsewhere (Oregon Department of Environmental Quality, 2010 [Appendix D]; Rounds and Sullivan, 2009, 2010). Briefly, that natural conditions model set Link River water quality on the basis of results from an Upper Klamath Lake model in which the Upper Klamath Lake TMDL was implemented. The same water-quality conditions for Link River were used as natural conditions water quality for the Lost River Diversion Channel and the Klamath Straits Drain. Point sources were removed from the natural conditions TMDL model. Keno Dam was left in place because historically a natural basalt structure was there (Oregon Department of Environmental Quality, 2010).

For the natural conditions model used in USGS modeling, instead of using output from an Upper Klamath Lake model to form the Upper Klamath Lake and Link River inflow conditions, Link River existing concentrations of orthophosphorus, algae, and organic matter for 2006–09 were decreased until the Upper Klamath Lake TMDL total phosphorus targets were met (Sullivan and others, 2011, p. 60). This is the same Link River boundary condition used in model scenarios 2 and 3(2a) and 3(2b), with the latter two described in this report. The total phosphorus inflow from this natural conditions model was higher than that of the TMDL natural conditions model in summer but still below the Upper Klamath Lake TMDL targets (fig. 2).

Rather than remove point sources for USGS natural conditions modeling, which would affect the residence time and complicate comparisons to scenarios that include the point sources, we retained those sources but set the concentration of all point-source inputs to the same concentration as the Klamath River where each inflow entered the river. The same was done for "nonpoint" tributaries such as the Klamath Straits Drain. To allow tributary inputs to be given concentrations that match those simulated in the river at their discharge location, the CE-QUAL-W2 code was modified, specifically in the wqconstituents.f90 source file (see appendix). A similar code change was made for water temperature in the temperature.f90 source file.

Finally, the natural conditions scenario was set up so that tributaries would distribute flow equally into all layers of the receiving stream (input TRC="DISTR") instead of weighted depending on water density in the layer; with the same temperature and concentration in the tributary and segment, water density would be the same and water would enter all layers equally. This modified CE-QUAL-W2 code was used to run only the natural conditions scenario.

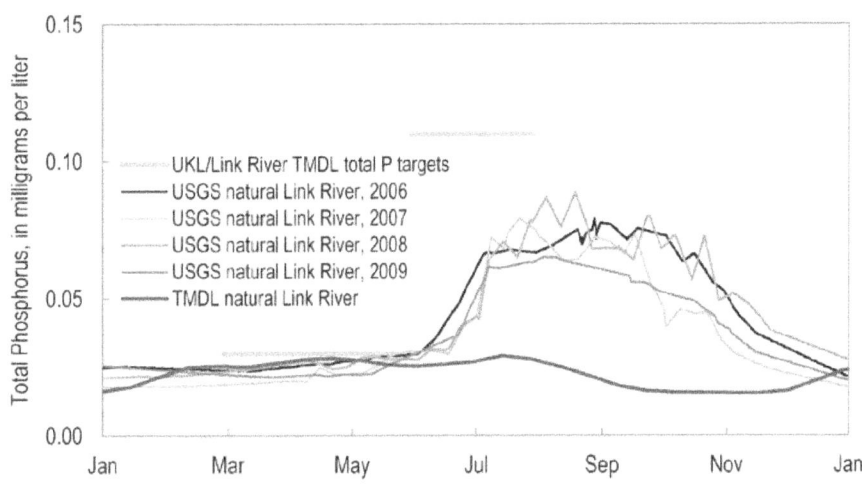

Figure 2. Graph showing Upper Klamath Lake and Link River total phosphorus TMDL targets and natural conditions Link River total phosphorus for the USGS and TMDL models.

Scenario Setup

Scenario 3 consists of the natural conditions scenario 3(nc) as well as model runs 3(1a), 3(1b), 3(2a), and 3(2b) that are identical to those completed for scenarios 1 and 2 (table 1). Those model runs were constructed as described in Sullivan and others (2011). To summarize, model runs for this scenario set included:

3(nc)   Natural conditions

Upper Klamath Lake at Upper Klamath Lake TMDL targets; point and nonpoint tributary sources set equal to Klamath River concentrations

3(1a)   Base case (same as scenario 1a)

All inflows at current conditions

3(1b)   TMDL tributaries (same as scenario 1b)

Link River at current conditions; point and non-point tributary sources at Klamath River TMDL allocations

3(2a)   TMDL Link River (same as scenario 2a)

Link River at Upper Klamath Lake TMDL targets; point and nonpoint tributary sources at current conditions

3(2b)   TMDL Link River and tributaries (same as scenario 2b)

Link River at Upper Klamath Lake TMDL targets; point and nonpoint tributary sources at Klamath River TMDL allocations

9

All scenarios were run with the USGS model for calendar years 2006–09 and the non-natural scenario results were compared to the relevant dissolved oxygen standard. Standards compliance was checked at the seven ODEQ compliance locations for all years. A compliance analysis also was conducted for the entire Link to Keno reach for year 2007 to determine whether the seven compliance locations were a representative subset of the entire reach.

Results of Scenario 3 Analyses

Depth-Averaged vs. Volume-Averaged Dissolved Oxygen Concentrations

During the winter and early spring, when little vertical variation in dissolved oxygen was present in the water column, depth-averaged and volume-averaged dissolved oxygen concentrations were almost identical (fig. 3). During late spring, summer, and fall, when vertical variations in dissolved oxygen concentrations in the water column were more common, differences between the depth-averaged and volume-averaged dissolved oxygen concentration were apparent, with the depth-averaged concentrations typically less than the volume-averaged concentrations. The differences occurred in the hourly values as well as the 7-day and 30-day values.

At the seven ODEQ compliance locations, differences between depth-averaged and volume-averaged concentrations were greatest at the most upstream compliance location (model segment 4) for all 4 years, up to a maximum of about 4 mg/L for hourly values in summer. At that location in summer, large algal populations produced supersaturated oxygen conditions near the water surface, and organic matter decomposition led to low dissolved oxygen concentrations near the bottom. The notable difference between surface and bottom dissolved oxygen concentrations led to the associated differences in results from the two calculation methods. Cross-sectional segment geometries also play a role in the difference between depth-averaged and volume-averaged concentrations. In addition to segment 4, summer differences in depth-averaged and volume-averaged concentrations at other compliance locations also occurred, ranging from near zero to 2 mg/L (for example, fig. 3).

Depth-averaged concentrations typically were lower than volume-averaged concentrations of dissolved oxygen, mainly because the depth-averaged method gives more weight to layers near the channel bottom, which most often had the lowest concentrations of dissolved oxygen. Only for limited times and a few locations did the depth-averaged calculation method produce higher dissolved oxygen concentrations than the volume-averaged calculation method. This occurred under the specific condition when a tributary inflow had both higher dissolved oxygen and a higher water density (based on temperature and concentration) compared to the river. Because of the higher density, the high dissolved oxygen tributary water would plunge to the channel bottom at the inflow segment; this unusual condition was an anomaly in the comparison of the two averaging methods.

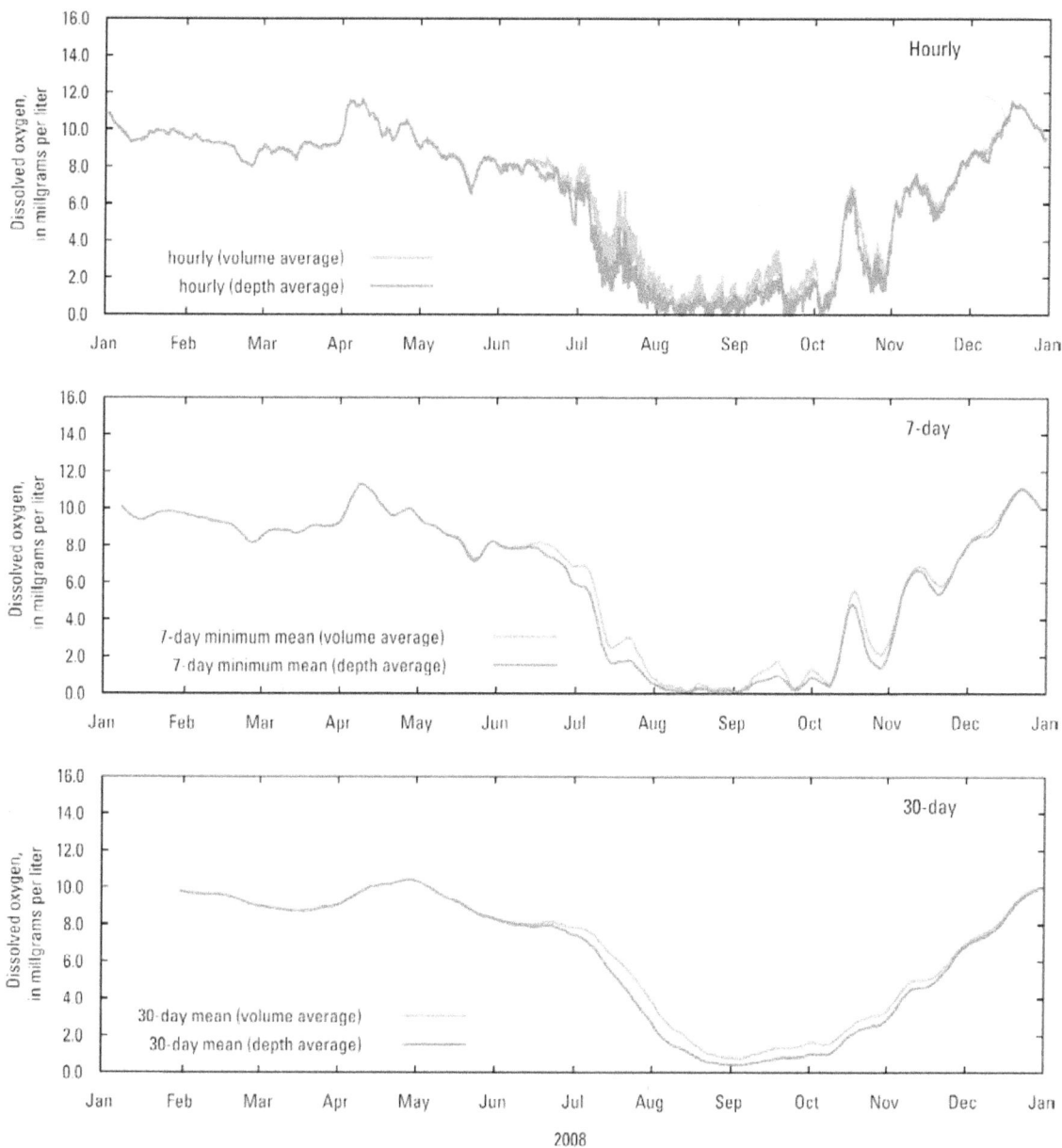

Figure 3. Graphs showing comparison of volume-averaged and depth-averaged dissolved oxygen concentration for calendar year 2008 at model segment 38, the Miller Island monitoring site.

Based on the comparative analysis, volume-averaged concentrations were used through the rest of this study because that calculation method provides a more appropriate representation of the average dissolved oxygen concentration when the entire cross section is considered. This may change in future analyses, and vertical profile measurements in the field may be easier to compare to results from the depth-averaged method. In any case, the differences between the averaging methods are notable and the selected method

should be documented when comparisons to the dissolved oxygen standard are made.

Natural Conditions Dissolved Oxygen Effect on the Standard

In general, the natural conditions dissolved oxygen concentrations were greater than the hourly, 7-day minimum mean, or 30-day mean dissolved oxygen standards. However, there were certain periods in summer, at certain locations, where the dissolved oxygen concentration

11

from the natural conditions run was lower than the numeric criteria. For example, at Miller Island the natural conditions dissolved oxygen concentration was less than all three criteria for certain periods in summer (fig. 4). When this occurred, the natural conditions dissolved oxygen concentration was set as the dissolved oxygen standard, with the applicable compliance metric set to the new standard with an additional reduction of 0.20 mg/L to account for the 0.20 mg/L anthropogenic allowance.

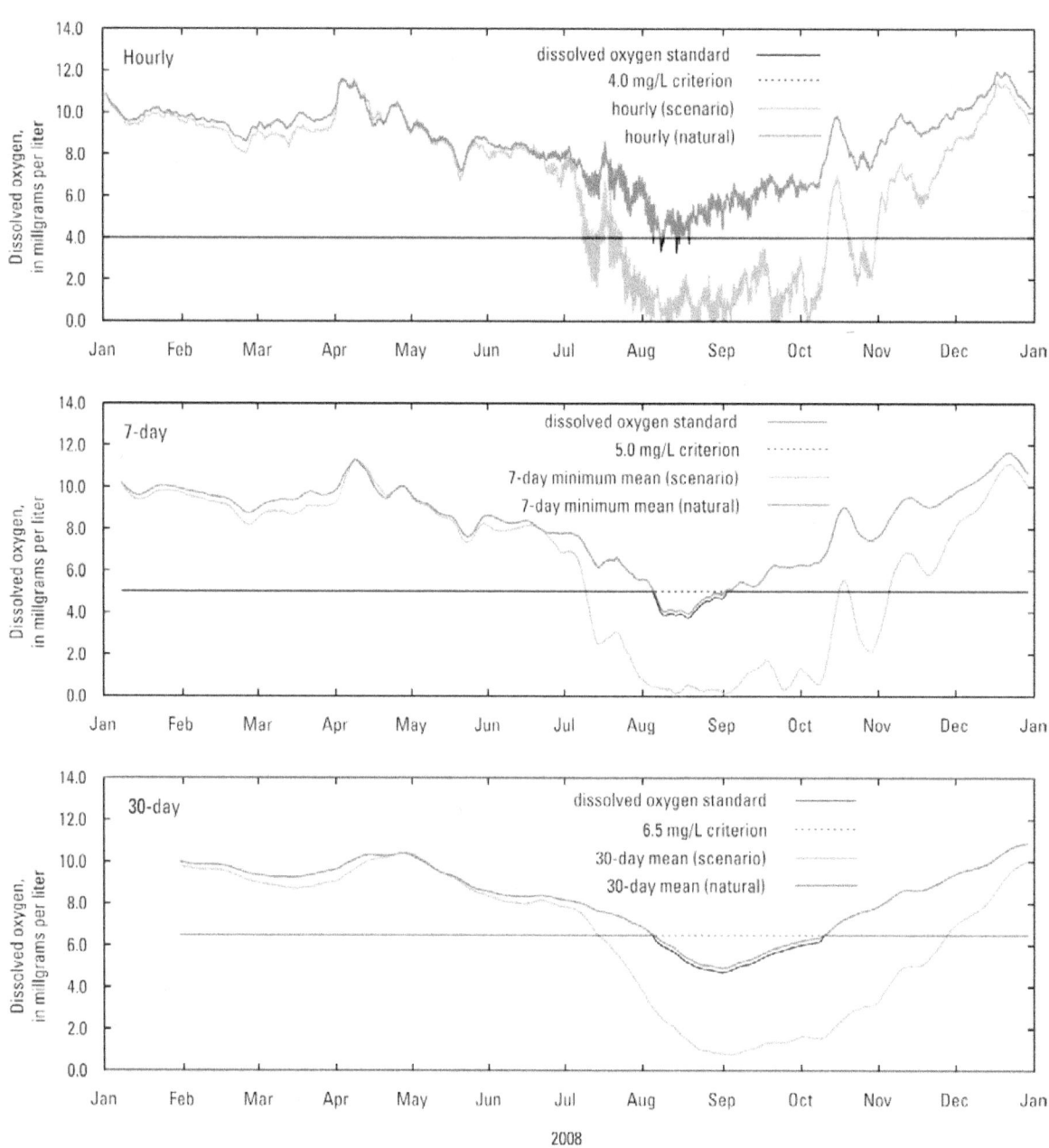

Figure 4. Graphs showing base case [3(1a)] and natural conditions [3(nc)] scenarios for 2008 dissolved oxygen concentration at Miller Island (model segment 38) in the Link River to Keno reach of the Klamath River, and the relevant dissolved oxygen standards.

Comparison to the Dissolved Oxygen Standard

For all scenario 3 model runs, for all years, the simulated Link to Keno dissolved oxygen concentration was above the dissolved oxygen standard for most of the winter and early spring (for example, fig. 4). At that time of year, the river contains less decomposable (oxygen-consuming) material, temperature-dependent decay rates are slower, and the cold water temperatures were able to retain higher levels of dissolved oxygen (higher solubility). However, during summer, the opposite condition occurred, with elevated levels of labile particulate organic matter, higher decay rates from temperature-dependent processes, and warmer temperatures decreasing the solubility of oxygen in water. The result was that during summer, violations of the dissolved oxygen standard occurred more frequently.

Of the three dissolved oxygen standards (instantaneous (hourly), 7-day minimum mean, 30-day mean), the hourly standard was violated least often, and the 30-day standard was violated most often. The maximum number of days that any of the three standards were violated, for a specific location and year, are presented in table 2; this was most often the number of days that the 30-day standard was violated. This summary table does not show how close the value was to the standard, only whether it was violated. In some cases, the value was close to the standard, but still in violation.

Table 2. Number of days the Klamath River would violate dissolved oxygen standards at the seven ODEQ compliance locations for base case and TMDL compliance scenarios for years 2006–(

[Abbreviations: KF, Klamath Falls wastewater treatment plant; SSSD, South Suburban wastewater treatment plant; LRDC, Lost River Diversion Channel; KSD, Klamath Straits Drain; seg, model segment; TMDL, total maximum daily load]

Scenario number and description		Days violating dissolved oxygen standard at compliance locations							
		Total for the 7 compliance locations	KF inflow	SSSD inflow	LRDC inflow	Miller Island	KSD inflow	KRS12a	Keno
			seg 4	seg 8	seg 19	seg 38	seg 69	seg 78	seg 95
2006									
3(1a)	Base case (current conditions)	676	24	75	89	120	122	122	124
3(1b)	TMDL tributaries	664	24	74	88	119	119	119	121
3(2a)	TMDL Link River	246	0	0	0	0	82	80	84
3(2b)	TMDL Link River and tributaries	117	0	0	0	0	65	48	4
2007									
3(1a)	Base case (current conditions)	729	53	89	105	119	121	122	120
3(1b)	TMDL tributaries	707	53	89	104	116	117	117	111
3(2a)	TMDL Link River	147	0	0	0	0	68	64	15
3(2b)	TMDL Link River and tributaries	113	0	0	0	0	67	46	0

Table 2. Number of days the Klamath River would violate dissolved oxygen standards at the seven ODEQ compliance locations for base case and TMDL compliance scenarios for years 2006–09—continued

[Abbreviations: KF, Klamath Falls wastewater treatment plant; SSSD, South Suburban wastewater treatment plant; LRDC, Lost River Diversion Channel; KSD, Klamath Straits Drain; seg, model segment; TMDL, total maximum daily load]

Scenario number and description		Days violating dissolved oxygen standard at compliance locations							
		Total for the 7 compliance locations	KF inflow	SSSD inflow	LRDC inflow	Miller Island	KSD inflow	KRS12a	Keno
			seg 4	seg 8	seg 19	seg 38	seg 69	seg 78	seg 95
2008									
3(1a)	Base case (current conditions)	833	67	92	113	134	141	142	144
3(1b)	TMDL tributaries	828	67	92	113	133	140	141	142
3(2a)	TMDL Link River	152	0	0	0	19	20	37	76
3(2b)	TMDL Link River and tributaries	38	0	0	0	19	19	0	0
2009									
3(1a)	Base case (current conditions)	854	80	102	120	133	139	139	141
3(1b)	TMDL tributaries	850	80	102	120	133	138	138	139
3(2a)	TMDL Link River	245	0	0	0	1	68	86	90
3(2b)	TMDL Link River and tributaries	80	0	0	0	1	62	16	1

Base case conditions, scenario 3(1a), violated the dissolved oxygen standard for some period of days at all seven ODEQ compliance locations for all 4 years that were simulated. For the same locations, 2006 and 2007 had the fewest violation days, and 2008 and 2009 had the most. A distinct spatial trend also was evident in the base case scenarios, with the fewest violation days on the upstream end and the highest number of violation days on the downstream end of the reach. This spatial trend is also illustrated in figure 5 (top), which shows the lowest 30-day mean

dissolved oxygen concentration for year 2007 for all of the 102 modeled segments. This trend is likely due to the fact that inflowing water from Link River generally has dissolved oxygen concentrations above 6.5 mg/L, but as waters move downstream, concentrations decrease because of oxygen demand from settling and decomposing algae, organic matter, and sediment oxygen demand. Further, there are additional inputs of oxygen-demanding material and/or low dissolved oxygen water from point and nonpoint sources throughout the reach.

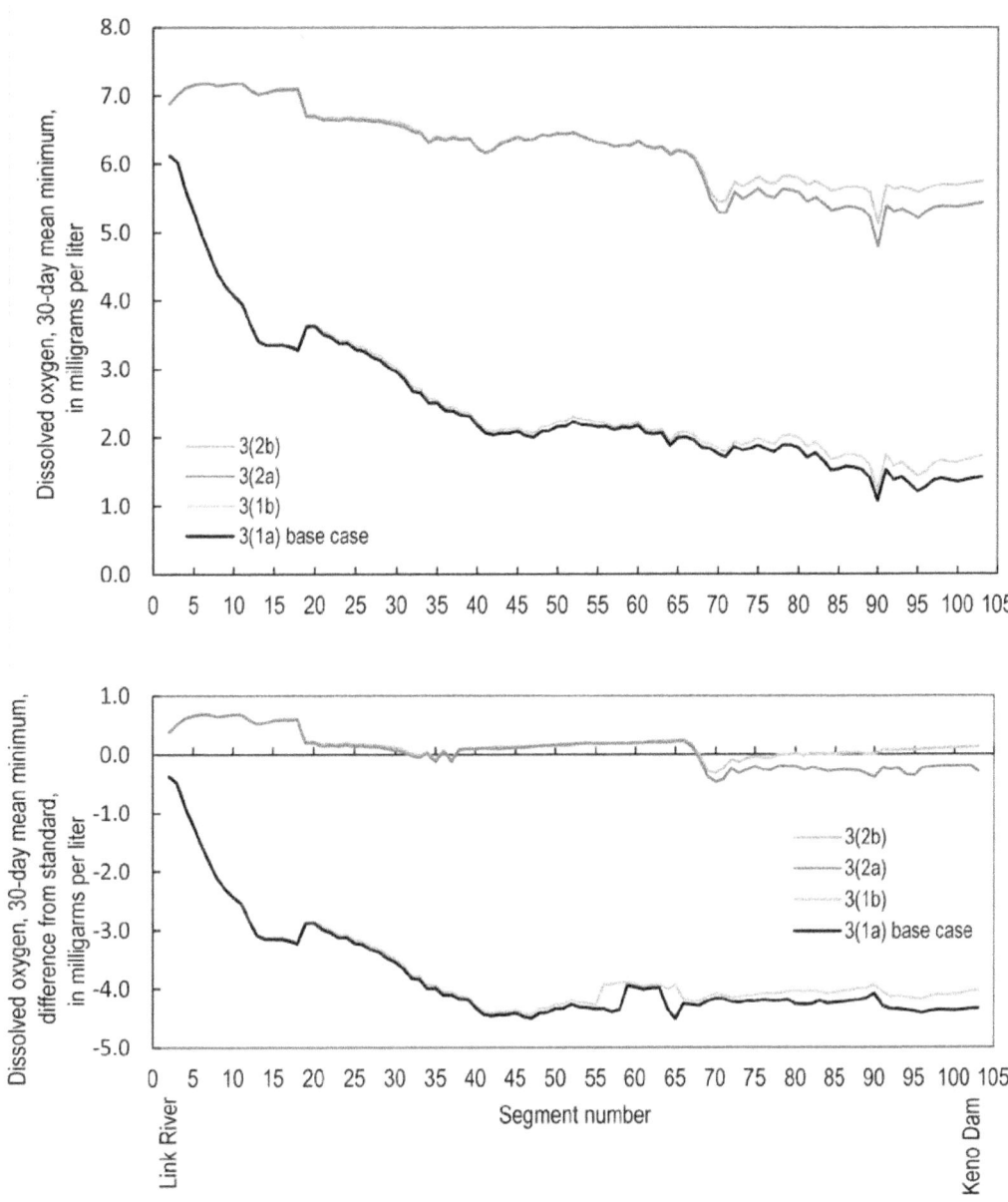

Figure 5. Graphs showing (A) minimum 30-day mean dissolved oxygen concentration at each modeled location during 2007 for scenario 3 model runs and (B) the difference between that minimum 30-day mean dissolved oxygen and the dissolved oxygen standard relevant for that location and day.

Setting the four point and nonpoint sources to their TMDL allocations in scenario 3(1b) by reducing inflowing concentrations of orthophosphate, organic matter, and algae by 59 to 95 percent (with some additional reductions in nitrate and ammonia) (Sullivan and others, 2011) did not substantially reduce the number of violation days compared to the base case 3(1a) at any of the seven ODEQ compliance locations (table 2). Compared to the base case, the point of

greatest improvement in 30-day mean dissolved oxygen was downstream of the point and nonpoint inflows (table 2; fig. 5, top). Considering the compliance locations, the greatest improvement was only nine fewer violation days at Keno in 2007 (8 percent). For all compliance locations and depending on the year, the number of dissolved oxygen violation days for scenario 3(1b) decreased 1 to 3 percent from current conditions.

Setting the Link River inflow to meet the Upper Klamath Lake TMDL water-quality targets in scenario 3(2a) had the largest effect of any of the scenario-3 model runs on Upper Klamath River dissolved oxygen concentrations (fig. 5), decreasing the number of violation days by 24 to 132 days compared to the base case 3(1a), depending on location (table 2). The improvement in meeting dissolved oxygen standards occurred throughout the reach, but was most notable in the upstream part of the reach. The most upstream compliance locations (segments 4, 8, and 19) had zero days violating the dissolved oxygen standard in this scenario for all years; segments farther downstream also had far fewer violation days. Considering all compliance locations and depending on the year, the number of dissolved oxygen violation days in scenario 3(2a) decreased 64–82 percent from current conditions.

Under conditions where Link River met its TMDL allocation 3(2a), the additional condition of setting nonpoint and point sources to meet their Klamath River TMDL allocations in scenario 3(2b) had a greater effect for downstream segments than the model runs in which Link River was set to current conditions (scenario 3(1b) versus 3(1a)) (table 2, fig. 5). With Link River at Upper Klamath Lake TMDL water-quality targets, dissolved oxygen through the reach was much closer to the standard, so small improvements could more easily move dissolved oxygen concentrations above the standard. With Link River at current conditions, the river was well below the standard, so small improvements from the point and nonpoint sources had a much smaller effect towards meeting the standard (fig. 5, bottom). Considering all compliance locations and depending on the year, the number of dissolved oxygen violation days in scenario 3(2b) decreased 83–95 percent from current conditions.

Several conclusions can be drawn from thes scenario results. First, assuming Link River to meet Upper Klamath Lake TMDL targets in scenarios 3(2a) and 3(2b) goes a long way towards meeting dissolved oxygen standards in the Link to Keno reach. None of the other actions tested in scenario 3 could pull the river into compliance with the dissolved oxygen standard if the Link River inflow was allowed to remain at its current condition (scenarios 3(1a) and 3(1b)). The importance of the Upper Klamath Lake and Link River boundary on the water quality of this reach has been documented previously (Oregon Department of Environmental Quality, 2010; Sullivan and others, 2011). Second, point and nonpoint sources meeting TMDL allocations had the greatest effect when the Link River inflow was already meeting Upper Klamath Lake water-quality targets. Finally, these scenarios also show that the effect of setting the Link River input to Upper Klamath Lake TMDL water-quality targets may have the greatest effect not at the inflow point, but further downstream (fig. 5). The point of maximum impact from these changes may even be downstream of Keno Dam. The downstream improvement arises from the fact that organic matter, algae, ammonia, and other oxygen demanding substances take time to decay, and the location of greatest change depends on decay rates, water velocity, travel time, and other factors.

Representativeness of the Seven ODEQ Compliance Locations

A comparison of the maximum number of days violating the dissolved oxygen standard for all model segments as well as the seven ODEQ compliance segments are shown in figure 6. These results indicate that the seven compliance locations selected by ODEQ appear to be a representative subset of dissolved oxygen compliance conditions in this reach of the Upper Klamath River. As with other analyses in this report, this will be re-examined after model updates for pH buffering and macrophyte growth are finalized. Although these segment locations appear to be representative for dissolved oxygen, similar analyses to determine the representativeness of these locations will be completed for other constituents and measures, such as ammonia toxicity and pH, which currently are out of compliance with water-quality standards.

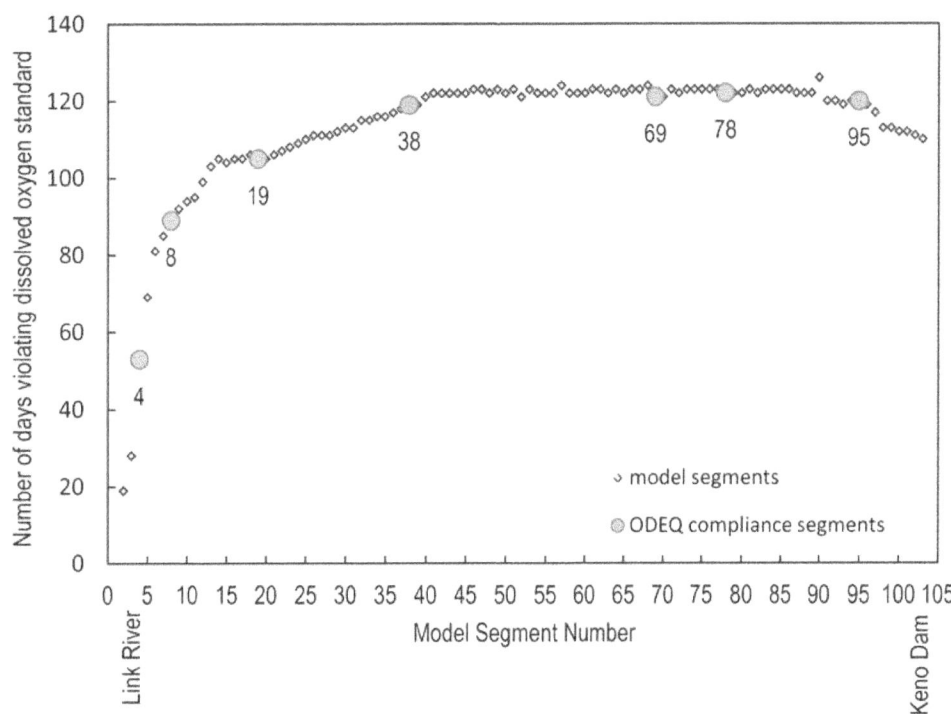

Figure 6. Graph showing number of days dissolved oxygen concentrations at all modeled locations in the Link River to Keno Dam reach violated the dissolved oxygen standard in the 2007 base case (scenario 1a). The seven segments where the Oregon Department of Environmental Quality monitors compliance with water-quality standards are noted.

Scenario 4. Comparison of the USGS and TMDL Models Using 2006–09 Data

In addition to the USGS model of the Link to Keno reach, an earlier CE-QUAL-W2 model was constructed by Tetra Tech and used as the technical basis for the Klamath River TMDL allocations (Tetra Tech, Inc., 2009). The development of the TMDL model for the years 2000 and 2002 did not have the benefit of the extensive field data and experimental research conducted in this reach for the USGS model in 2006–09. Reviews of the TMDL model questioned the concentration and partitioning of organic matter used in that model as well as other assumptions (Rounds and Sullivan, 2009, 2010). The TMDL model and the USGS model of this reach cannot be compared directly because the models were set up to simulate different years. To assess qualitative differences between output from the two models and eva-

luate the effects of several important model factors, scenario 4 was developed wherein the TMDL model executable, control file parameters and rates, bathymetry, and organic matter partitioning assumptions were applied with the 2006–09 flow, water quality, and meteorological input files. The 2006–09 dataset was selected for the main comparison because it is more extensive than the 2000 and 2002 datasets used by the TMDL model.

Scenario Setup

To apply the TMDL model for this scenario, the 2006–09 model input files were used, including flow, temperature, water quality, and meteorology, with some adjustments to make those inputs consistent with the assumptions built into the TMDL model. The partitioning of organic matter in the water-quality input files, for example, was changed to match that of the TMDL model. While the 2006–09 input files for the USGS model included both labile (quickly decaying) and refractory (slowly decaying) organic matter, the TMDL model inputs had zero refractory organic matter and had low concentrations of dissolved organic matter (Rounds and Sullivan, 2009, 2010). To change the organic matter partitioning in the 2006–09 input files so it was consistent with the rates and assumptions built into the TMDL model, a total organic-matter concentration was calculated from the sum of labile and refractory, dissolved and particulate organic matter concentrations (LDOM+RDOM+LPOM+RPOM). Then, the organic matter was partitioned according to the partitioning assumptions used by the TMDL model. For example, Link River organic matter inputs were partitioned into 20 percent labile dissolved organic matter and 80 percent labile particulate organic matter, with no refractory organic matter, either dissolved or particulate.

Several other changes were made to the 2006–09 input files in this scenario so that they more closely matched the setup of the TMDL model input files. The separate 2006–09 sluice, fish ladder, and spill gate outflows at Keno Dam were added together to produce only one outflow. Further, the TMDL model did not differentiate between algal groups, so the concentration of diatoms, blue-green algae, and "other" algae used by the USGS model were added together to produce one algae input. In addition, precipitation input files were used for both the USGS and TMDL models in this scenario to keep hydrologic inputs the same. Precipitation had not been explicitly used in the earlier 2000 and 2002 TMDL model simulations, but were used in the USGS model.

The TMDL model executable, graph file, shade file, bathymetry file, and control files were used without substantive modification to preserve the rates, parameters, shading, and river geometry of the original TMDL model. The TMDL model executable was a modified version of CE-QUAL-W2 version 3.12, whereas the USGS model used CE-QUAL-W2 version 3.6. Most of the TMDL control file parameters were not changed; however, the wind height parameter

was changed to 10 m to match the height of the wind sensor where the 2006–09 meteorological data were measured. In addition, evaporation as part of the water budget (not the heat budget) had been turned off in the TMDL model, but was turned on for these scenarios; this change is small and unimportant to the results, but is more consistent with the water balance used for the 2006–09 datasets.

The results of this application of the TMDL model to the 2006–09 inputs were compared to measured data and to results from the calibrated USGS models. This comparison provides a qualitative means to examine the effect of differences in organic matter partitioning (labile versus refractory, dissolved versus particulate), algae algorithms, model parameter values, bathymetry, and the nature of the sediment oxygen demand (zero order only in the TMDL model versus a combination of zero and first order in the USGS model). This comparison is not meant to provide a means to criticize either the TMDL model or the USGS model, but simply to evaluate how different approaches to formulating certain boundary conditions and different methods of simulating certain river processes can result in different model predictions. In this way, the comparison is best used to highlight which processes or assumptions have a large effect on model results so that our understanding of the importance of these factors and the sensitivity of models to them can be improved. However, it is important to remember that this scenario is only a partial comparison and this analysis focuses on base case, current condition models; it does not compare the setup of the natural conditions model for the TMDL process, which included different assumptions than the natural conditions USGS model, as noted in scenario 3.

Results of Scenario 4 Analyses

Qualitative comparison of the scenario 4 TMDL model to the calibrated 2006–09 USGS model and measured data (figs. 7a, 7b) shows large differences for certain constituents and only minor differences for others. Because the general nature of the differences was similar between years, only year 2007 results are included in this report. Despite the different algorithms used to simulate algae in the TMDL model and the USGS model, the spatial and temporal patterns in the modeled algae populations were similar between the two models (fig. 7a). Total nitrogen and ammonia concentrations were underpredicted in summer from Miller Island to

Keno in the TMDL model, and nitrate concentrations were overpredicted compared to data in summer from KRS12 to Keno. The overprediction of nitrate in the downstream end of the reach had been noted during reviews of the TMDL model (Rounds and Sullivan, 2009, 2010).

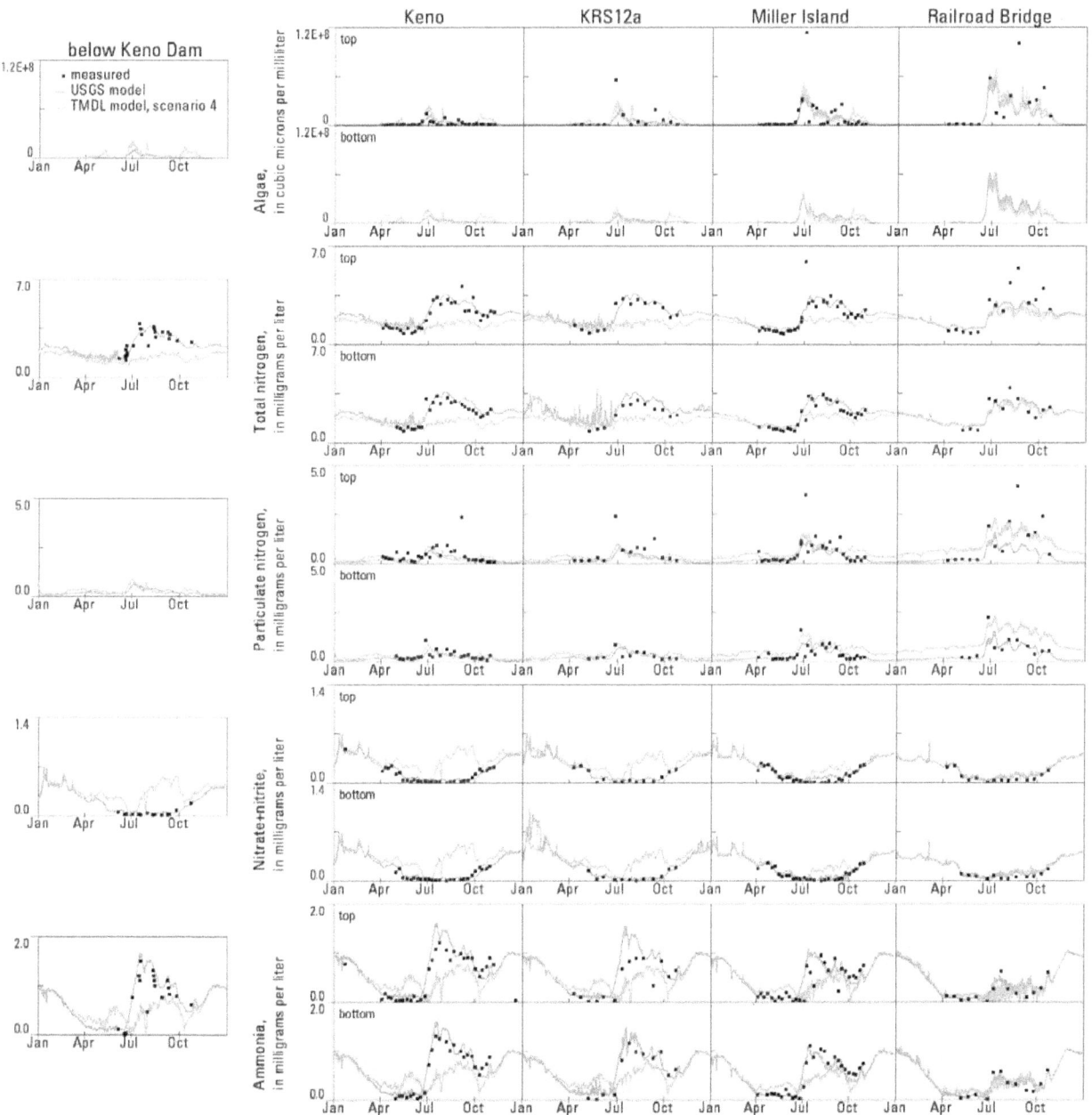

Figure 7a. Graphs showing comparison of year 2007 measured algae, total nitrogen, particulate nitrogen, nitrate, and ammonia data, calibrated model results, and scenario 4 (2007 inputs applied to TMDL model setup) results for sites in the Klamath River upstream of Keno Dam, Oregon.

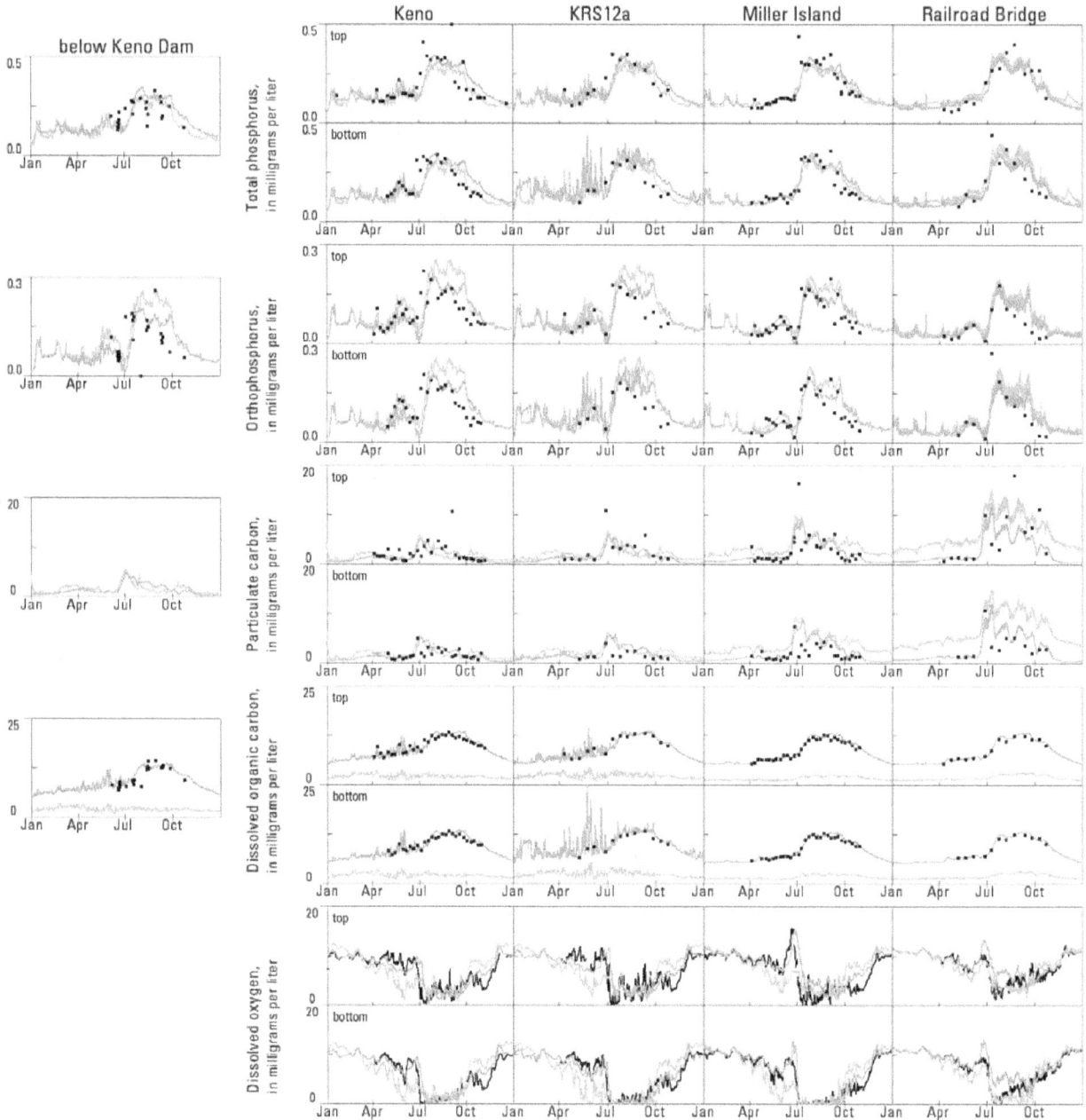

Figure 7b. Graphs showing comparison of year 2007 measured total phosphorus, orthophosphorus, particulate organic carbon, dissolved organic carbon, and dissolved oxygen data, calibrated model results, and scenario 4 (2007 inputs applied to TMDL model setup) results for sites in the Klamath River upstream of Keno Dam, Oregon.

Spatial and temporal patterns of orthophosphorus and total phosphorus concentrations were similar between the TMDL and USGS models, with perhaps a slight overprediction of orthophosphorus by the TMDL model in summer at KRS12a and Keno and slight overprediction of total phosphorus by the USGS model at the same locations and times (fig. 7b). Particulate carbon in the scenario 4 TMDL model was notably high in winter compared to measured data at the upstream end of the Link-Keno reach (fig. 7b); differences decreased in the downstream direction. The disappearance of particulate matter from upstream to downstream was due in part to

20

the fact that all organic matter in the TMDL model was classified as labile (quickly decaying). Dissolved organic matter concentrations showed large differences between the two models, with concentrations greatly underpredicted by the scenario 4 TMDL model, but this is understandable because the data collected in 2006–09 indicate a different organic matter partitioning than the assumptions used by the TMDL model in 2000 and 2002, which did not have the benefit of a more robust organic matter dataset.

The implications of the TMDL model representations of particulate organic matter were manifest in the dissolved oxygen concentrations. The oxygen demand associated with particulate organic matter in the TMDL model application that was classified as completely labile also led to dissolved oxygen concentrations that were too low during spring in the scenario 4 TMDL model. Recovery of dissolved oxygen in the fall also was sooner than measured data or the USGS model with the scenario 4 TMDL model. This is likely because the TMDL model uses only a zero-order sediment oxygen demand that does not keep track of demand from settled organic material and, as a result, is not responsive to seasonal changes other than that from water temperature; the USGS model represents part of the sediment oxygen demand with a first-order process that includes the effect of that seasonally deposited material. On the other hand, the TMDL model was able to more accurately capture the low dissolved oxygen concentrations at the Railroad Bridge site in summer. It is hoped that further model comparisons for other years will reveal more opportunities to learn from models that were calibrated with different datasets and different sets of assumptions.

This analysis revealed several constituents where different algorithms, rates, and assumptions did not make a notable difference in model predictions for 2006–09. For example, both models predicted algae, orthophosphorus, and total phosphorus concentrations to have similar magnitudes and seasonal patterns at many locations. On the other hand, the analysis also confirmed several issues that are critical to un-

derstanding and representing the dynamics and patterns of Klamath River water quality. In particular, organic matter in this system is best represented by a mixture of relatively labile particulate material and a substantial concentration of relatively refractory dissolved material, and a zero-order-only sediment oxygen demand does not capture the seasonal and relatively dynamic effect of settled algal and particulate organic material. To assess the effect of future management activity, models should aim to capture the pertinent processes as accurately as possible. The USGS model will continue to be used for this ongoing scenario work.

Scenario 5. Shunting Particulate Material from Diversion Canals into the Klamath River

Scenario 5 examined the effects on Klamath River water quality under conditions where particulate material was "shunted," or diverted, from Klamath Project withdrawal points back to the river such that particulate material stayed in the Klamath River system and out of the canals. Another goal of this particulate shunting analysis is to understand whether keeping particulate matter out of the Klamath Project diversion canals and the Lost River basin would decrease nutrient and organic matter in the Lost River Diversion Channel and Klamath Straits Drain enough to move them towards their TMDL allocations. Future analyses will examine the second question more closely. Results presented here focus on how particulate shunting might affect Klamath River dissolved oxygen concentrations and compliance with dissolved oxygen standards.

Under current operations, four Klamath Project diversion canals take water from Link River and the Upper Klamath River upstream of Keno Dam; the withdrawn water is routed into Reclamation's Klamath Project and the Lost River basin. These diversion canals are the A Canal, the Lost River Diversion Channel, North Canal, and Ady Canal (fig. 1). The Lost River Diversion Channel typically withdraws water to the Lost River in summer and returns flow to the Klamath River during the rest of the year. The other three diversion canals act only as withdrawals (fig. 8); the A Canal withdrew the largest amount of water during 2006–09 compared to the other three canals. The particulate material under consideration included all three types of algae, labile and refractory particulate organic matter, and inorganic suspended sediment.

Withdrawals in this scenario were essentially filtered within the model to keep particulate matter out of the diversion canals. Flows were not altered in this scenario. Scenarios were run for all 4 years, 2006–09.

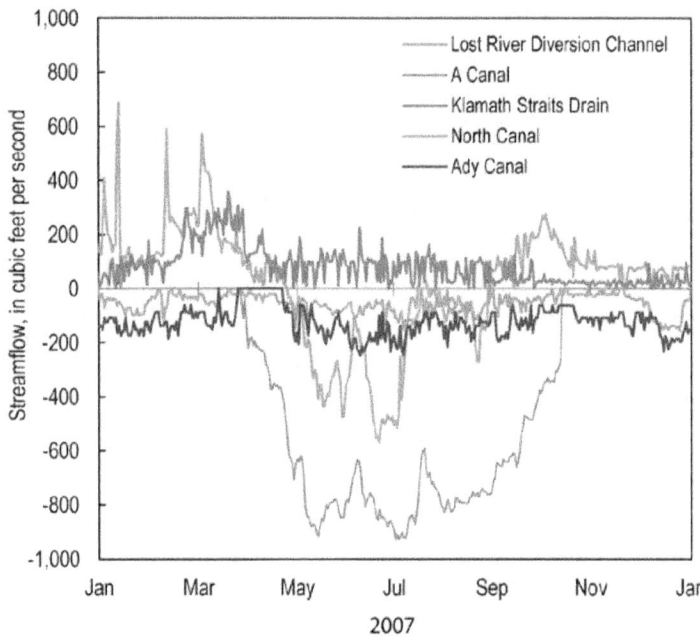

Figure 8. Graph showing flows for A Canal, Lost River Diversion Channel, North Canal, Ady Canal, and Klamath Straits Drain for 2007. Diversions away from the Klamath River system are shown as negative flows; flows to the Klamath River from the Lost River basin are shown as positive flows. For comparison, flows at the upstream end of this Klamath River reach, at Link River, averaged 1,165 cubic feet per second in 2007.

Particulate Shunting

The shunting of particulate material from A Canal was accomplished outside the model, as the A Canal takes water from upstream of the model's upper boundary. The A Canal technically withdraws water from a southern lobe of Upper Klamath Lake upstream of Link River Dam. Because the A Canal intake is fairly close to the dam, which is the main outlet of the lake, it was assumed that the water quality at the A Canal intake was similar to water quality at the mouth of Link River. The shunted mass of inorganic suspended sediment, labile particulate organic matter, refractory particulate organic matter, blue-green algae, diatoms, and other algae were individually calculated based on concentrations at the mouth of Link River and

A Canal flows. For the years modeled, A Canal diversions only occurred between late March and mid-October (for example, fig. 8). It was assumed that all particulates shunted from the A canal intake flowed into Link River, and that travel time was negligible between the A Canal intake and the Link River model boundary. For each type of particulate material, the shunted mass of A Canal particulates was added to the mass of particulates used in base-case model scenarios at Link River, and new Link River particulate concentrations were calculated from the masses and the Link River flow. For example, the sum of the particulate organic load (LPOM+RPOM+BlueGreen algae+Diatoms+Other algae) at Link River with and without shunting in 2006 is shown in figure 9.

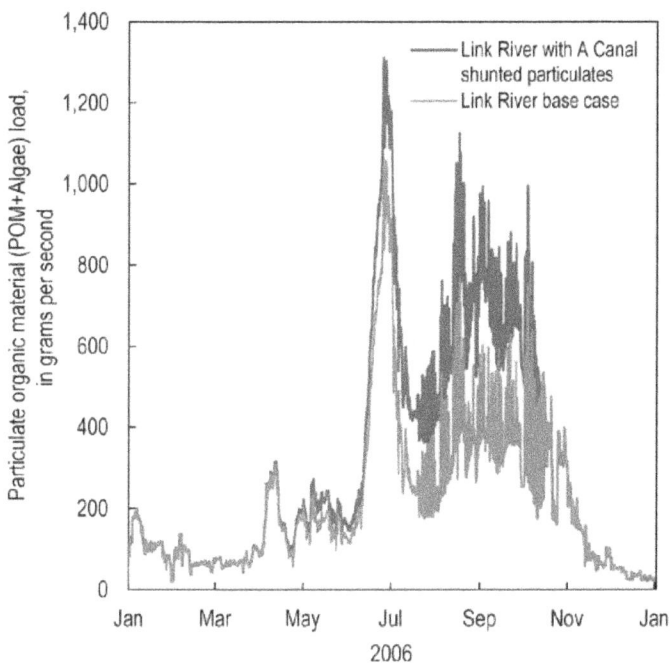

Figure 9. Graph showing particulate organic load (particulate organic material + algae) at Link River for 2006 under current conditions and under A Canal particulate shunting.

For the three in-reach diversions (Lost River Diversion Channel, North Canal, and Ady Canal), particulate shunting was accomplished within the model by changing the CE-QUAL-W2 code so all that particles remained in the Klamath River at selected diversions (see appendix). Mass balance calculations during code development checked that the increase in particulate matter at the relevant Klamath River segments matched the decrease in particulate matter in the diversion outflow.

Changes to Return-Flow Concentrations

Return flows in the Link-Keno reach were dominated by contributions from the Lost River basin. The Lost River system is a complex 90-mile series of riverine segments, reservoirs, drains, canals, and wetlands (Tetra Tech, Inc., 2005). Water returns from the Lost River basin to the Upper Klamath River via the Lost River Diversion Channel (part of the year) and the Klamath Straits Drain (fig. 8). If particulate material did not enter the Lost River basin from the Klamath Project diversion canals, it is possible that return flows to the Klamath River from the Lost River basin would have lower concentrations of particulate matter and possibly dissolved material because forms of nutrients and organic matter could be transformed within the Lost Riv-

er system. Due to the complexity of the Lost River system, which also includes Tule Lake and the Lower Klamath National Wildlife Refuge, it is difficult to estimate precisely how Lost River Diversion Channel and Klamath Straits Drain return-flow concentrations might change. Given this uncertainty, a bracketing approach was applied, with two end members and an intermediate condition for the return-flow concentrations. Model runs for this scenario included:

5a.   Particulates shunted at diversions. No change to Lost River Diversion Channel or Klamath Straits Drain return concentrations. (End member)

5b.   Particulates shunted at diversions. Intermediate change to Lost River Diversion Channel and Klamath Straits Drain nutrients, algae, and organic matter concentrations.

5c.   Particulates shunted at diversions. Dissolved oxygen concentrations set to saturation, and zeroed out concentrations of particulate and dissolved nutrients, algae, and organic matter for the Lost River Diversion Channel and Klamath Straits Drain returns. (End member)

Each of the end member runs (5a, 5c) is unlikely to occur individually, but their inclusion allows for the examination of the entire range of possible results.

23

The intermediate condition (5b) for Lost River Diversion Channel return-flow concentrations was estimated by reducing Lost River Diversion Channel algae, nutrients, and organic matter concentrations (both dissolved and particulate) by 0–50 percent, depending on how much the organic mass load was reduced at A Canal by particulate shunting; a 0-percent reduction was applied when no particulate shunting was occurring, and a 50-percent reduction was applied at maximum shunting. Concentrations were proportionately reduced for intermediate shunting values. The 50 percent maximum was an estimate for this scoping exercise. Due to the configuration of the Lost River–Upper Klamath River systems, Lost River Diversion Channel return flows would only be affected by changes to the A Canal diversions, as the other three diversions are further downstream. Both particulate and dissolved concentrations were reduced in the return-flow concentrations because *Aphanizomenon flos-aquae* (AFA), which makes up most of the Upper Klamath Lake algae in summer, has been found to decay quickly in the Klamath River (Sullivan and others, 2010); decay releases dissolved nutrients and organic matter, so removal of AFA would likely decrease dissolved nutrients and organic matter also.

The intermediate condition (5b) for Klamath Straits Drain return-flow concentrations was estimated by reducing Klamath Straits Drain algae, nutrients, and organic matter concentrations (both dissolved and particulate) by up to 50 percent, depending on how much the organic mass load was reduced at A Canal, as described above. In addition, a minimum 10-percent reduction was instituted throughout each calendar year. The Klamath Straits Drain is farther downstream from the A Canal diversion; however, water quality would also be affected by reduced particulate loading from the Lost River Diversion Channel, North Canal, and Ady Canal, the latter two of which withdraw water throughout the year (fig. 8).

The formulation of the intermediate condition for this scenario is only an estimate and subject to a great deal of uncertainty. To accurately formulate an intermediate reduction scenario, more information would be needed about travel time as well as the spatial and temporal dynamics of organic matter and nutrient transformations within the Lost River basin, including Tule Lake and the Lower Klamath National Wildlife Refuge. Collecting such data is outside the scope of this study, so only estimates were formulated for the intermediate scenario (5b). Should more information become available, it could be combined with existing knowledge about the system (for example, Risley and Gannett, 2006), and the formulation of this intermediate scenario could be revised.

Results of Scenario 5 Analyses

In all years, and at all seven ODEQ compliance locations, shunting particulate material away from the Klamath Project diversion canal intakes and into the Klamath River (scenarios 5a, 5b, 5c) led to more days where dissolved oxygen standards in the Klamath River were violated compared to the current conditions base case (table 3). The number of days during which dissolved oxygen standards would be violated increased from an additional 10 to an additional 78 days, depending on location, year, and scenario details. Considering all compliance locations and depending on the year, the number of dissolved oxygen violation days in scenario 5a, 5b, and 5c increased 24 to 32 percent from current conditions.

Table 3. Number of days the Klamath River would violate dissolved oxygen standards at the seven ODEQ compliance locations in the base case and particulate shunting scenarios for years 2006–09.

[Abbreviations: KF, Klamath Falls wastewater treatment plant; SSSD, South Suburban wastewater treatment plant; LRDC, Lost River Diversion Channel; KSD, Klamath Straits Drain; seg, model segment; TMDL, total maximum daily load; OM, organic matter; DO dissolved oxygen]

Scenario number and description		Days violating dissolved oxygen standard at compliance locations							
		Total for the 7 compliance locations	KF inflow	SSSD inflow	LRDC inflow	Miller Island	KSD inflow	KRS12a	Keno
			seg 4	seg 8	seg 19	seg 38	seg 69	seg 78	seg 95
2006									
	Base case (current conditions)	*676*	24	75	89	120	122	122	124
5a	Shunt, LRDC and KSD current	*894*	102	120	126	131	137	138	140
5b	Shunt, LRDC and KSD intermediate	*894*	102	120	126	131	137	138	140
5c	Shunt, LRDC and KSD zero OM, nutrients, and algae, with DO at saturation	*883*	102	120	126	130	134	135	136
2007									
	Base case (current conditions)	*729*	53	89	105	119	121	122	120
5a	Shunt, LRDC and KSD current	*949*	98	119	130	141	151	153	157
5b	Shunt, LRDC and KSD intermediate	*948*	98	119	130	141	151	153	156
5c	Shunt, LRDC and KSD zero OM, nutrients, and algae, with DO at saturation	*930*	98	119	128	139	146	148	152
2008									
	Base case (current conditions)	*833*	67	92	113	134	141	142	144
5a	Shunt, LRDC and KSD current	*1065*	95	123	144	165	179	179	180
5b	Shunt, LRDC and KSD intermediate	*1065*	95	123	144	165	179	179	180
5c	Shunt, LRDC and KSD zero OM, nutrients, and algae, with DO at saturation	*1051*	95	123	142	162	175	176	178
2009									
	Base case (current conditions)	*854*	80	102	120	133	139	139	141
5a	Shunt, LRDC and KSD current	*1100*	100	123	137	157	192	193	198
5b	Shunt, LRDC and KSD intermediate	*1100*	100	123	137	157	192	193	198
5c	Shunt, LRDC and KSD zero OM, nutrients, and algae, with DO at saturation	*1060*	100	123	136	155	180	180	186

The formulation of the Lost River Diversion Channel and Klamath Straits Drain return-flow concentrations (5a, 5b, 5c) had little effect on Upper Klamath River dissolved oxygen compliance in this scenario. Even between the end members, with unchanged water quality (5a) or zero organic matter, nutrients, algae, and dissolved oxygen at saturation (5c), the numbers of days violating the dissolved oxygen standard on-

ly increased by 1 to 5 percent, depending on the year. The difference in simulated dissolved oxygen concentrations between the end member scenarios was more striking on a seasonal basis in winter (fig. 10); however, dissolved oxygen concentrations were well above the standard at that time.

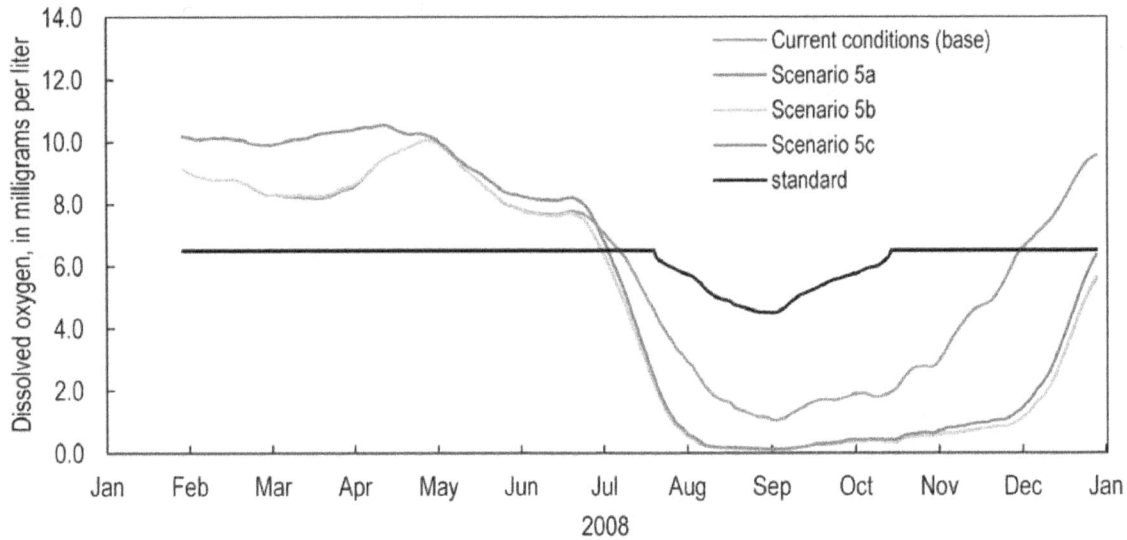

Figure 10. Graph showing 30-day mean dissolved oxygen concentrations at model segment 78 (site KRS12a) for the base case and scenarios 5a, 5b, 5c, and 5d in 2008. The relevant dissolved oxygen standard is also shown.

Several factors contribute to the lack of effect of the return-flow composition on Upper Klamath River dissolved oxygen compliance. First, the Lost River Diversion Channel return-flow concentration was only affected by A Canal particulate shunting for a short period of time during conditions when both the Lost River Diversion Channel flowed towards the Klamath River (mostly in winter) and the A Canal was withdrawing (summer) (fig. 8). Also, while the other return-flow canal, Klamath Straits Drain, did flow into the Klamath River all year, it was noted in the scenario 3 analysis that changes to point and nonpoint sources had relatively small effects on Upper Klamath River dissolved oxygen concentrations when Link River loads were high. In any case, even though the differences between runs 5a and 5c can be quantified and

might be important under some circumstances, the effects are small in terms of the dissolved oxygen budget under scenario 5 conditions.

This scenario demonstrates the importance of the diversion canal operation on Upper Klamath River water quality. If particulate matter is not withdrawn and the particulate is shunted back to the Klamath River, then dissolved oxygen conditions in the river would worsen. It is of course possible that shunted material could be removed from the river as part of the shunting process; in this case there would be no change to Klamath River particulate loading at the diversion locations during shunting, but some improvements in Klamath River dissolved oxygen conditions might result from improved water quality in the return flows.

Future model scenarios will examine the effects of not only changing water quality in the diversion canals, but the effect of changing flows as well. Future runs will also include an analysis of the effects of particulate shunting on compliance with water-quality standards for parameters other than dissolved oxygen.

Acknowledgments

Funds for this study were provided by the Bureau of Reclamation. Discussions with Jason Cameron, Rick Carlson, and Jessica Asbill-Case (Reclamation) were helpful at various stages of the project. The authors are grateful to Dan Turner (Oregon Department of Environmental Quality) for his helpful discussions of the dissolved oxygen standard and sharing ideas for post-processing of model output.

References Cited

Bureau of Reclamation, 2005, Natural flow of the Upper Klamath River—Phase I: Accessed March 22, 2012, at *http://www.usbr.gov/mp/ kbao/docs/undepleted_klam_fnl_rpt.pdf*.

Cole, T.M., and Wells, S.A., 2008, CE-QUAL-W2—A two-dimensional, laterally averaged, hydrodynamic and water-quality model, version 3.6: U.S. Army Corps of Engineers, Instruction Report EL-08-1 [variously paged].

Deas, M.L., and Vaughn, J., 2011, Keno Reservoir particulate study 2008—Technical memorandum, Prepared for the Bureau of Reclamation, Klamath Basin Area Office, April 2011: Davis, Calif., Watercourse Engineering, Inc., 38 p.

Mrazik, S., 2007, Oregon water quality index summary report, water years 1997–2006: Oregon Department of Environmental Quality, DEQ07-LAB-007-TR, 13 p.

Oregon Department of Environmental Quality, 2007, Oregon's 2004/2006 integrated report: Accessed November 16, 2007, at *http://www.deq.state.or.us/wq/assessment/rpt0 406.htm*.

Oregon Department of Environmental Quality, 2010, Upper Klamath and Lost River subbasins total maximum daily load (TMDL) and water quality management plan (WQMP): Accessed March 22, 2012, at *http://www.deq.state.or.us/WQ/TMDLs/ klamath.htm*.

Oregon Department of Environmental Quality, 2011, Oregon Administrative Rules OAR 340-041: Oregon Secretary of State Archives, accessed October 21, 2011, at *http://arcweb.sos.state.or.us/pages/rules/oars_ 300/oar_340/340_041.html*.

Poulson, S.R., and Sullivan, A.B., 2010, Assessment of diel chemical and isotopic techniques to investigate biogeochemical cycles in the Upper Klamath River, Oregon, USA: Chemical Geology, v. 269, no. 1–2, p. 3–11.

Risley, J.C., and Gannett, M.W., 2006, An evaluation and review of water-use estimates and flow data for the Lower Klamath and Tule Lake National Wildlife Refuges, Oregon and California: U.S. Geological Survey Scientific Investigations Report 2006–5036, 18 p. (Also available at *http://pubs.er.usgs.gov/ publication/sir20065036*.)

Rounds, S.A., and Sullivan, A.B., 2009, Review of Klamath River total maximum daily load models from Link River Dam to Keno Dam, Oregon: U.S. Geological Survey Administrative Report, 37 p., accessed April 13, 2012, at *http://or.water.usgs.gov/proj/keno_reach/down load/klamath_river_model_review_final.pdf*.

Rounds, S.A., and Sullivan, A.B., 2010, Review of revised Klamath River total maximum daily load models from Link River Dam to Keno Dam, Oregon: U.S. Geological Survey Administrative Report, 32 p., accessed April 13, 2012, at *http://or.water.usgs.gov/proj/ keno_reach/download/ klamath_model_rereview_final.pdf*.

Sullivan, A.B., Deas, M.L., Asbill, J., Kirshtein, J.D., Butler, K., and Vaughn, J., 2009, Klamath River water quality data from Link River Dam to Keno Dam, Oregon, 2008: U.S. Geological Survey Open-File Report 2009–1105, 25 p. (Also available at *http://pubs.er.usgs.gov /publication/ofr20091105*.)

Sullivan, A.B., Deas, M.L., Asbill, J., Kirshtein, J.D., Butler, K., Wellman, R.W., Stewart, M.A., and Vaughn, J., 2008, Klamath River water quality and acoustic Doppler current profiler data from Link River Dam to Keno Dam, 2007: U.S. Geological Survey Open-File Report 2008–1185, 24 p. (Also available at *http://pubs.er.usgs.gov/publication/ofr20081185.*)

Sullivan, A.B., Rounds, S.A., Deas, M.L., Asbill, J.R., Wellman, R.E., Stewart, M.A., Johnston, M.W., and Sogutlugil, I.E., 2011, Modeling hydrodynamics, water temperature, and water quality in the Klamath River upstream of Keno Dam, Oregon, 2006–09: U.S. Geological Survey Investigations Report 2011–5105, 70 p. (Also available at *http://pubs.er.usgs.gov/publication/sir20115105.*)

Sullivan, A.B., Snyder, D.M., and Rounds, S.A., 2010, Controls on biochemical oxygen demand in the Upper Klamath River, Oregon: Chemical Geology, v. 269, no. 1–2, p. 12–21.

Tetra Tech, Inc., 2005, Model configuration and results Lost River model for TMDL development—Prepared for U.S. Environmental Agency Regions 9 and 10, Oregon Department of Environmental Quality, and North Coast Regional Water Quality Control Board: Portland, Oregon [variously paged], accessed April 13, 2012, at *http://www.epa.gov/region9/water/tmdl/lost-river/AppendixATmdlModelReport-8-29-05.pdf.*

Tetra Tech, Inc., 2009, Klamath River model for TMDL development—Prepared for U.S. Environmental Agency Regions 9 and 10, Oregon Department of Environmental Quality, and North Coast Regional Water Quality Control Board: 196 p., accessed May 20, 2011, at *http://www.deq.state.or.us/wq/tmdls/docs/klamathbasin/uklost/KlamathLostAppendixC.pdf.*

Watercourse Engineering, Inc., 2004, Klamath River modeling framework to support the PacifiCorp Federal Energy Regulatory Commission Hydropower Relicensing Application, March 9, 2004: Davis, California, 291 p.

Weddell, B.J., 2000, Relationship between flows in the Klamath River and Lower Klamath Lake prior to 1910—Report to U.S. Fish and Wildlife Service, Klamath Basin National Wildlife Refuges, Tulelake, California: Pullman, Washington, 12 p.

Appendix—Code Changes to CE-QUAL-W2

To formulate the executable for the natural conditions and particulate shunting model runs, the following changes were made to the CE-QUAL-W2 source code (version 3.6 from the November 2010 release). The original source code can be downloaded at *http://or.water.usgs.gov/proj/keno_reach/models.html*

All code was compiled as described in the CE-QUAL-W2 manual (Cole and Wells, 2008) with the addition of the /fp:precise switch to force consistency in floating-point calculations.

A. Natural Conditions Code Changes

1. Changed code in temperature.f90 for tributary inputs

```
IF (TRIBUTARIES) THEN
  DO JT=1,JTT
   IF (JB == JBTR(JT)) THEN
    I = ITR(JT)
    IF (I < CUS(JB)) I = CUS(JB)
    DO K=KTTR(JT),KBTR(JT)
     IF (QTR(JT) < 0) THEN
       TSS(K,I) = TSS(K,I) +T2(K,I)*QTR(JT)*QTRF(K,JT)
       TSSTR(JB) = TSSTR(JB)+T2(K,I)*QTR(JT)*QTRF(K,JT)*DLT
     ELSE
       TSS(K,I) = TSS(K,I) +T2(K,I)*QTR(JT)*QTRF(K,JT)         ! SR 9/08/11
       TSSTR(JB) = TSSTR(JB)+T2(K,I)*QTR(JT)*QTRF(K,JT)*DLT      ! SR 9/08/11
       ! TSS(K,I) = TSS(K,I) +TTR(JT)*QTR(JT)*QTRF(K,JT)        ! SR 9/08/11
       ! TSSTR(JB) = TSSTR(JB)+TTR(JT)*QTR(JT)*QTRF(K,JT)*DLT     ! SR 9/08/11
     END IF
    END DO
    VOLTRB(JB) = VOLTRB(JB)+QTR(JT)*DLT
   END IF
  END DO
END IF
```

2. Changed code in wqconstituents.f90 for tributary inputs

```
IF (TRIBUTARIES) THEN
  DO JT=1,JTT
   IF (JB == JBTR(JT)) THEN
    I = ITR(JT)
    IF (I < CUS(JB)) I = CUS(JB)
    DO K=KTTR(JT),KBTR(JT)
     IF (QTR(JT) < 0.0) THEN
       CSSB(K,I,JC) = CSSB(K,I,JC)+C1(K,I,JC)*QTR(JT)*QTRF(K,JT)
     ELSE
       CSSB(K,I,JC) = CSSB(K,I,JC)+C1(K,I,JC)*QTR(JT)*QTRF(K,JT)   ! SR 08/26/11
       ! CSSB(K,I,JC) = CSSB(K,I,JC)+CTR(JC,JT)*QTR(JT)*QTRF(K,JT)   ! SR 08/26/11
     END IF
    END DO
   END IF
  END DO
END IF
```

B. Particulate Matter Shunting Code Changes

1. Changed code in endsimulation.f90 to accommodate FILTER_PARTICLES variable

```
DEALLOCATE (HYDRO_PLOT, SEDIMENT_RESUSPENSION, FILTER_PARTICLES)
```

2. Changed code in input.f90 to handle the new FILTER_PARTICLES variable

```
ALLOCATE (IWD(NWDT), KWD(NWDT), QWD(NWDT), EWD(NWDT), KTW(NWDT), KBW(NWDT),
FILTER_PARTICLES(NWDT))
FILTER_PARTICLES = IWD < 0                              ! SR 08/08/11
IWD = ABS(IWD)                                          ! SR 08/08/11
```

3. Changed code in outputa.f90 to show filtered withdrawals correctly

```
IF (.NOT. FILTER_PARTICLES(JWD) .OR.                                      &
 ( CN(JC) /= NPSI .AND. CN(JC) /= NLPOM .AND. CN(JC) /= NRPOM .AND.       &
  CN(JC) /= NLPOMP .AND. CN(JC) /= NRPOMP .AND. CN(JC) /= NLPOMN .AND. CN(JC) /= NRPOMN .AND. &
  (CN(JC) < NSSS .OR. CN(JC) > NSSE ) .AND.                              &
  (CN(JC) < NAS  .OR. CN(JC) > NAE ) .AND.                               &
  (CN(JC) < NZOOS .OR. CN(JC) > NZOOE) )) THEN               ! SR 08/10/11
 CSUM(CN(JC)) = CSUM(CN(JC))+C2(K,IWD(JWD),CN(JC))*QSW(K,JWD)
END IF                                                    ! SR 08/10/11


IF (.NOT. FILTER_PARTICLES(JWD) .OR.                                    &
  ( CDN(JC,JWWD) == 1 .OR. CDN(JC,JWWD) == 4 .OR. CDN(JC,JWWD) == 9 .OR.  &
   CDN(JC,JWWD) == 16 .OR. CDN(JC,JWWD) >= 19 )) THEN          ! SR 08/11/11
 CDSUM(CDN(JC,JWWD)) = CDSUM(CDN(JC,JWWD))+CD(K,IWD(JWD),CDN(JC,JWWD))*QSW(K,JWD)
ELSE IF (CDN(JC,JWWD) == 3) THEN               ! filtered TOC = DOC       ! SR 08/11/11
 CDSUM(3) = CDSUM(3)+CD(K,IWD(JWD),1)*QSW(K,JWD)                  ! SR 08/11/11
ELSE IF (CDN(JC,JWWD) == 6) THEN               ! filtered TON = DON       ! SR 08/11/11
 CDSUM(6) = CDSUM(6)+CD(K,IWD(JWD),4)*QSW(K,JWD)                  ! SR 08/11/11
ELSE IF (CDN(JC,JWWD) == 7) THEN               ! filtered TKN = DON + NH4    ! SR 08/11/11
 CDSUM(7) = CDSUM(7)+(CD(K,IWD(JWD),4)+C2(K,IWD(JWD),NNH4))*QSW(K,JWD)     ! SR 08/11/11
ELSE IF (CDN(JC,JWWD) == 8) THEN               ! filtered TN = DON + NO3 + NH4  ! SR 08/11/11
 CDSUM(8) = CDSUM(8)+(CD(K,IWD(JWD),4)+C2(K,IWD(JWD),NNO3)+C2(K,IWD(JWD),NNH4))*QSW(K,JWD) ! SR
08/11/11
ELSE IF (CDN(JC,JWWD) == 11) THEN              ! filtered TOP = DOP        ! SR 08/11/11
 CDSUM(11) = CDSUM(11)+CD(K,IWD(JWD),9)*QSW(K,JWD)                ! SR 08/11/11
ELSE IF (CDN(JC,JWWD) == 12) THEN              ! filtered TP = DOP + PO4    ! SR 08/11/11
 CDSUM(12) = CDSUM(12)+(CD(K,IWD(JWD),9)+C2(K,IWD(JWD),NPO4))*QSW(K,JWD)        ! SR 08/11/11
END IF                                                    ! SR 08/11/11
```

4. Changed code in w2modules.f90 to declare FILTER_PARTICLES variable

```
LOGICAL, ALLOCATABLE, DIMENSION(:) :: FLUX, EVAPORATION, ZERO_SLOPE, FILTER_PARTICLES
```

5. Changed code in wqconstituents.f90 to do particulate shunting

```
IF (WITHDRAWALS) THEN
DO JWD=1,JWW
  IF (.NOT. FILTER_PARTICLES(JWD) .OR.                           &
   ( JC /= NPSI .AND. JC /= NLPOM .AND. JC /= NRPOM .AND.          &
    JC /= NLPOMP .AND. JC /= NRPOMP .AND. JC /= NLPOMN .AND. JC /= NRPOMN .AND. &
    (JC < NSSS .OR. JC > NSSE ) .AND.                            &
    (JC < NAS  .OR. JC > NAE ) .AND.                             &
    (JC < NZOOS .OR. JC > NZOOE) )) THEN                        ! SR 08/08/11
   IF (QWD(JWD) /= 0.0) THEN
    IF (JB == JBWD(JWD)) THEN
    I = MAX(CUS(JBWD(JWD)),IWD(JWD))
    FORALL(K=KTW(JWD):KBW(JWD))
     CSSB(K,I,JC) = CSSB(K,I,JC)-C1S(K,I,JC)*QSW(K,JWD)
    END FORALL
    END IF
   END IF
  END IF                                          ! SR 08/08/11
 END DO
END IF
```